Praise Less, Encourage More

Judge, Evaluate and Manipulate Less; Support, Fortify, Influence, Galvanize and Embolden More!

SunBurst Publications

Robert T. Tauber PhD

[KDP Praise Less Cis 7 13 21]

Learn the difference between praise and encouragement. Then, commit to using less of the former, and championing the latter.

Robert T. Tauber. PhD

Professor Emeritus
The Pennsylvania State University
rtt1453@comcast.net

Acknowledgements

This normally is where the author thanks all the people around him who have contributed to his modicum of success as a writer. No doubt these people exist, from parents, teachers, and coaches, to my wife of over 50 years, Cecelia, and my children, David and Rebecca. What, specifically, was their contribution? Although the exact opposite of what I am recommending in this book, most of what was offered, by everyone but my wife, consisted of praise in one form or another and not necessarily encouragement. Cecelia, on the other hand, executed *all* the behaviors listed later in this book that are synonyms for encouragement – bolster, buoy, spur, energize, galvanize, and impart resolution. I suppose that others in my life *would* have offered more encouragement and less praise if only they had first read this book.

At this point, it seems appropriate to announce, "See, I was praised a lot and I turned out OK!" The jury is still out on that claim. The bottom line, though, is just imagine what the outcome would have been if heavy doses of encouragement, instead of praise, had been offered by *all* of those around your author. Its outcome even scares the author, himself.

Imagine heavy doses of encouragement for your own life. Imagine it for those special people in your life. After reading this book, you may well realize what has been missing in your own life – an abundance of encouragement, but at least you now will be a better prepared to supply it in the lives of others. Read on.

Preface

To write is to sweat! To write is to throw your hat in the ring without any promise that it will end well. To write is to begin with high aspirations and end with more than just a dose of humility. To write is to start off blind about the length and difficulties of the road ahead. I suppose that not knowing all of this ahead of time is a blessing. If this were not the case, few would begin the journey at all. For me, this journey has been worth it. I hope that you agree.

To Get You in the Mood!

Every worthwhile endeavor or challenge requires a "warm-up." Whether we are talking about gymnastics, basketball, or dancing with the stars, or a game of chess, contestants must get both their mind and their body ready for what will follow.

It is said that a picture is worth a thousand words. This is most likely true. But really good quotations, from respectable sources far wiser than your author, can come in a close second. To get you in the mood for what follows, I have cited several quotations related to praise and encouragement for your review. Take a moment and let their messages sink in. Consider this a form of intellectual foreplay!

- "Flatter me, and I may not believe you. Criticize me and I may not like you. Ignore me and I may not forgive you. Encourage me, and I will not forget you."
  (–William Arthur Ward)

- "A word of encouragement during a failure is worth more than an hour of praise after success." Why bother praising someone who already feels praiseworthy?
  (–Unknown Author)

- "Correction does much, but encouragement does more." We seem good at the first, but not so good at the second.
  (–Johann Wolfgang von Goethe)

- "Note how good you feel after you have encouraged someone else. No other argument is necessary to suggest that [you should] never miss the opportunity to give encouragement."
  (–George Adams)

- "Praise the effort, not the result." Better still, encourage the entire ongoing process!
(–Jesse Itzler)

- "Praise, like gold and diamonds, owes its value only to its scarcity."
(–Samuel Johnson)

- "False praise is worse than no praise."
(–Felix Dennis)

- "Instruction does much, but encouragement does everything."
(–Johann Wolfgang von Goethe)

- "Be an encourager: When you encourage others, you boost their self-esteem, enhance their self-confidence, make them work harder, lift their spirits and make them successful in their endeavors."
(–Roy T. Bennett)

- "Remember, children need our encouragement all the time – not just when they have accomplished something adults find praiseworthy."
(–Gwen Dewar)

- "Friends, Romans, countrymen, lend me your ears. I come to bury Caesar, not to praise him…." In this *Julius Caesar* eulogy, Mark Antony, downplays the importance of praise.
(–Mark Antony)

Table of Contents

CHAPTER 1

CHAPTER 2

When Praise is Perceived as an Evaluation - 18

Praise: It is designed to manipulate!
Praise: Can be a sneaky way to flatter!
Praise: Most threatening aspect; remaining praiseworthy!
Praise: Increases psychological distance between two people!
Praise: Must be "handled," sometimes even "denied!"
Praise: Can elicit unwanted psychological reactions!

CHAPTER 3

A Preferred Alternative, Encouragement! - 60

CHAPTER 4

Praising when the Other Person *Does Not* Feel Praiseworthy! - 91

CHAPTER 5

Praising when the Other Person *Does* Feel Praiseworthy - 100

CHAPTER 6

Others Who Recognize the Cautions Behind Delivering Praise – 108

CHAPTER 1

"Nobody gets praised for the right reason."
[There always seems to be some hidden agenda!]
(–Diana Wynne Jones)

Introduction

I wanted to "hook" you as a reader right away and, hence, I thought I would begin by saying, "It was the best of times; it was the worst of times," repeating the first line of the Charles Dickens novel, *A Tale of Two Cities*. How does this famous line apply? I will argue that, believe it or not, praise often falls into the "worst" category, while encouragement *always* falls into the "best" category. I not only will make this argument I will convince from 85 percent to 90 percent of the readers who complete this book to pledge to stop, or significantly reduce, their use of praise and, instead, focus upon delivering encouragement.

Another reader "hook" that I considered using was, Mark Antony's eulogy "Friends, Romans, countrymen, lend me your ears. I come to bury Caesar not to praise him" (William Shakespeare, *Julius Caesar*, Act 3, Scene 2). Clearly, even Shakespeare saw the less attractive or less desirable side of praise.

I also could have tried to "hook" the reader by offering pithy, yet right on the money, quotations. Consider, "Nobody gets praised for the right reasons" (Diana Wynne Jones, *Castle in the Air*) or "Sweet words are like honey, a little may refresh, but too much, gluts the stomach" (Anne Bradstreet). The first quotation suggests that those who praise often have a hidden agenda. The second quotation suggests that too much praise can be damaging. Of note is the fact that it is impossible for there ever to be too much encouragement or that large quantities of it could ever be harmful.

Quotations can say so much that I have offered two more. "He who praises everybody praises nobody" (S. Samuel Johnson). This would be like everyone having diamonds. At that point diamonds would have little or no value. Like praise, their value lies in their scarcity. Encouragement, on the hand, can be offered to everyone, at any time, and in great quantities without losing any of its value.

"I know of no manner of speaking so offensive as that of giving praise and closing with an exception" (Richard Steele). This most offensive delivery often takes the form of, "You did a great job, BUT…" The praise was just a precursor to the real "BUT" message. This topic, and many others, will be discussed further in CHAPTER 2 that deals with the many "cautions in delivering praise."

Finally, I have tried to "hook" you, the reader, by offering little stories such as "Aurora's Story," or "Gene Hackman's Story." Everyone loves a good story. These short stories are first and foremost designed to help teach the concepts of praise and encouragement and to push for greater use of the latter. Second, they are designed to be just plain interesting, and there is nothing wrong with that.

IN CASE IT IS NOT OBVIOUS

In case it is not immediately obvious, your author believes that praise is fraught with danger and, as such, one should be cautious in its use. I hope that it is equally obvious that your author has offered an alternative to praise – that being encouragement.

Let's take a visit to your local doctor. You schedule an appointment and meet with your doctor because you have been experiencing some shoulder pain. What is the problem you wonder – a recent fall, arthritis, old age? At the end of your patient-doctor consultation you are told that the problem is likely arthritis, not uncommon among 77-year-olds like your author.

What is the cure? There isn't one. How, then, can I at least manage the debilitating pain associated with exaggerated and quick movements? Your physician offers two medicines in pill form to "treat" your arthritis. The dilemma is which medicine to take? Rather than use the children's rhymes approach of "eeny, meeny, miny, moe," often used to select who is "it" in a game of tag, you decide to make your decision in an informed, scientific manner. By this I mean, you decide to read the labels on the two pill containers. In particular you are interested in the possible negative side-effects, or adverse reactions, that by law must be identified.

First you read the list of negative side-effects associated with the pills in the first bottle. Possible side-effects, sometimes a lengthy list, usually are printed on the information that accompanies the medicine. Below are just some of the negative side-effects associated with taking the pills in the first bottle.

> "Taking these pills may cause: Nausea, Dizziness, Drowsiness, Fatigue, Rapid Heartbeat, Insomnia, Anxiety, Influenza, Bleeding, Dry Mouth, Blurred Vision, Muscle Aches & Pains, Ear Infections, Stomach Cramps, Constipation, Vomiting, Diarrhea, Depression, Headaches, Thoughts of Suicide, and even Death!"

At this point you might be thinking that it may be better to just live with the arthritis pain rather than take the chance on experiencing one or more of these negative side-effects. But, before you make your final decision, you go on to read the list of negative side-effects associated with the pills in the second bottle. Surprise! Surprise!

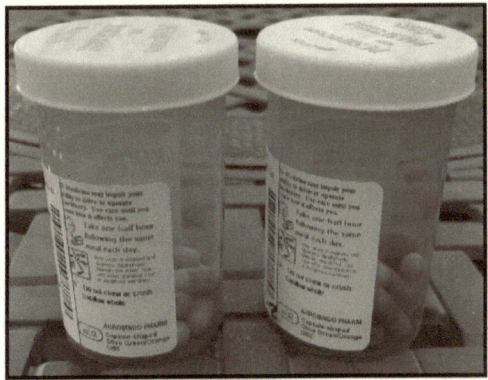

When you read the small print on the bottle and on the accompanying printed literature, possible negative side-effects are nowhere to be found! Is this simply an omission? No. Is it simply a misprint? No. At this point it becomes a no-brainer about which pills, those in Bottle #1 or those in Bottle #2, should be selected. The pills that have NO POSSIBLE NEGATIVE SIDE-EFFECTS are the clear winner. As you continue reading you will find an analogous situation between delivering praise and delivering encouragement. Once again, there will be a clear winner.

Let's be fair. It is not enough that I say that praise often has negative side-effects, but delivering encouragement has none! The evidence needs to "say so." That evidence is delivered in the 21 cautions against using praise that are presented in Chapter 2.

A SPECIAL CASE FOR PRAISING

I need to say the following right up front. This book is all about one person, usually someone of a higher rank or position, praising another person. The individual holding the higher rank or position exercises, via delivering or withholding praise, an element of control over the person being praised. We are *not* talking about that other use of the word, praise, where depending upon our choice of a deity, we might proclaim, as in *Psalms* 117:1-2, "Praise the

LORD, all you nations...." Here, the word praise is being used to extol or express admiration, not to evaluate. Clearly, no mortal man would believe that he or she is able to evaluate or judge his deity.

CONVERSATIONAL WRITING STYLE

This book is not written as, nor was it intended to be, primarily a piece of scientific literature, complete with an Abstract, Methods, Subjects, Results, and Conclusions. You will be spared all those elaborate and seemingly endless charts and graphs that often accompany scientific articles. These charts and graphs may have value but just not for my aim of getting you to praise less and encourage more.

You will find some personal stories of mine and of others that should help illuminate the difference between delivering praise and delivering encouragement. Hopefully, you will find this book reader-friendly and immediately useful!

SOUL SEARCHING

Before reading further, stop and do some soul searching. Ask yourself a few probing questions. There is no one looking over your shoulder nor is anyone listening in judgment to your responses. It is just you and your conscience. The bottom line here is that before you can move forward with the topic, *Praising Less, Encouraging More*, you first must establish some sort of baseline for where you currently stand. Then, it will be possible to measure any change that you might experience with respect to your use of praise and encouragement.

Why do you praise people? Five simple words. Think of someone, a son or daughter, a husband or wife, a friend, neighbor or colleague, a sibling or parent, and recall an instance or two when you delivered a praise statement. To your son or daughter, you might have said, "Great job, I am really proud of you." Or, you might simply have said, "Wow, that's tremendous." To your spouse or good friend, you might have delivered a compliment (i.e., praise) regarding their outfit – "That dress looks wonderful on you," "That tie looks just perfect with that shirt," or "These cinnamon buns are outstanding."

One assumes that you, like all human beings, unless incapacitated for some reason by say alcohol or drugs, have a reason for doing what you do, for saying what you say, and saying it when you say it. Having a reason for delivering your praise suggests that you have a motive for delivering that praise. So, once again, why do you praise people? What is your motive for praising them? If you answer, "I have no motive" then it suggests that praise (or, for that matter, encouragement) words or statements simply dribble out of your mouth.

My mother and father, when just married, lived with my father's parents. So, I am told, my grandmother would regularly and profusely praise my mother's cooking of scrambled eggs. It wasn't until much later that my mother, Katherine, realized just why her mother-in-law lavished praise on her scrambled eggs. You guessed it. Grandma was more than happy to relinquish the repeated chore of cooking scrambled eggs for the family breakfast. She had a motive for her praise.

Why do you think that people praise you? Now here is where it gets personal! Might they have an ulterior motive? Or, do their praise and encouragement words just leak out of their mouths. Probably, they have a motive for their praise. So, when a boyfriend says to his girlfriend, "That blouse looks really great on you," what is his motive, what does he want? Be careful, I know what some of you are thinking! Perhaps there are some boyfriends who don't have any ulterior motives at all. Trust me, they are the exception. More than likely he wants something, even if it is only to get her to wear more blouses just like this one because it gives him pleasure. There is nothing kinky here, it is just human nature. We tend to praise what we value! The boyfriend praises what he deems worthy of praising.

APPLES AND ORANGES

My first goal is to convince you that apples are apples and oranges are oranges. Apples and oranges, although both fruits, *are not* synonyms for each other. In the same vein, praise is praise and encouragement is encouragement. They, too, are not synonyms for each other. Further, praising is not a way to encourage!

This book is an effort to persuade you to use more encouragement and less praise – it is just that simple. To accomplish this, then, I will need to share with you the well documented cautions that exist surrounding the use of praise. The more that you realize the damage that praising can deliver, the easier it will be for you to be accept substituting encouragement.

HAND ME THE WATCHAMACALLIT!

Envision an operating room where the surgeon asks for a scalpel. He calls to the nurse, "Hand me the whatchamacallit." The nurse hesitates and seems confused. The surgeon says, "You know, hand me the thingamajig!" Still the nurse stands there almost paralyzed. Out of frustration the surgeon yells, "Hand me the doohickey!" What is the problem here? The problem is that two people are trying to communicate but are unsuccessful. The problem here is that the patient might expire while they try to communicate. What would be helpful would be if both parties called the same thing by the same name.

Things have names. That is the basis of having a common language. Just because YOU call something, something, does not make it so! Your author did not make it that way. Society did, it is the final arbitrator of what something is called. Society creates dictionaries in order to help. Hence, praise has one definition and encouragement has a different definition. Look it up if you don't believe me. People unaware of the defined difference between these terms often end up calling something, say, encouragement when, in fact, it is praise – and vice versa. For us to have an intelligent discussion, one of productive give and take, we simply must have what your author calls a "participant's" language. We must agree to abide by society's definitions for the terms that we use. Praise and encouragement can be no exception.

WHAT PERCENT OF EACH CAUTION DO YOU ACCEPT?

Although as the author I am the one pounding out the computer keys, what I offer is not simply a collection of my ramblings or personal opinions. All of what is presented in this book flows from the educational and psychological literature. In other words what is presented here can be backed up in the scientific, testable, literature. This book presents sound theory and effective practice – both necessary tools for parents, professionals, practitioners and more. I hope that you agree.

You will be asked at the conclusion of each of the cautions for using praise to stick your neck out and indicate on a 0% to 100% scale how convincing each caution was. It should prove interesting to see which cautions offered were the most persuasive. It will also be interesting to see if collectively the cautions sway you enough to either stop, or significantly reduce, using praise and, instead, substitute the use of encouragement.

THREE SITUATIONS; BEING CAUTIOUS IN DELIVERING PRAISE

- Praising when praise is perceived as an evaluation!
- Praising when the other person *does not* feel praiseworthy!
- Praising when the other person *does* feel praiseworthy!

Chapter 2 focuses primarily on the 1st situation where we, as caring and supportive people, too readily deliver statements of praise to those who perceive praise as an evaluation. Chapter 3 offers a preferred alternative response, encouragement. Chapter 4 and Chapter 5 address the 2nd and 3rd situations where one *does not* or *does* feel praiseworthy. Chapter 6 consists of a set of annotated references that view the need for caution when supplying praise.

CHAPTER 2

"Stop giving meaningless praise and start giving meaningful action."
(–Steve Maraboli)

When praise is perceived as an evaluation

A LIST OF CAUTIONS

The following offers specific cautions in delivering praise. Before you are ready to come after me with a baseball bat for challenging the use of praise, please hear me out. Keep in mind that later I will be offering a more powerful alternative to praise – encouragement.

You don't have to buy, lock-stock-and-barrel, each of the following cautions to delivering praise. But if you accept even portions of the case made for each of the cautions, collectively these portions may add up to a convincing argument for being cautious in delivering praise, especially when there is a more viable alternative in the form of delivering encouragement!

1ˢᵗ *caution!*

Praise: It is designed to manipulate!

The puppet master's only concern is how well they can manipulate their marionettes.
–Steven Redhead
The sweetest of all sounds is praise.
–Xenophon
Praise underserved is satire in disguise.
–Henry Broadhurst

First and foremost, praise is designed to manipulate – whether intended or not intended it still manipulates. It is the single most popular tool of a behaviorist (think B. F. Skinner's behaviorism). It is the "carrot" in Skinner's "carrot and stick" approach. It is the primary tool used by those who endorse "behavior modification." Perhaps the sweetness of its sound allows many to be manipulated.

When you deliver praise, you may not intend your message to be an evaluation, but if that is how it is interpreted by the receiver then that is what it is – manipulation! This goes to reinforce just how actually powerless those who rely on praise delivery as a purposeful tool of manipulation are. They can send any thought-to-be-praise messages they like, but it is up to the receiver to determine the impact of those messages. It is sort of like the saying, "It is in the eye of the beholder" (e.g., receiver).

As an opening exercise to this praise caution, I ask an audience, "How many of you, unless you are a bit unusual, just love to be manipulated?" Sure, an occasional person in the back of the room will say "yes," generating brief snickers and laughs. But, in fact, no one seriously raises his hand in support of being manipulated. My exercise goes on by asking the audience, "If you don't like to be manipulated, then what makes you think that others like to be manipulated?" At this point the audience limits their eye contact with me and with fellow audience members. The impact of answering this question honestly is sobering.

The exercise continues still more. The audience is asked, "How many of you have your life completely in order?" Yep, that same person in the back of the room who responded favorably to being manipulated says "I do" to my life completely in order question. Fewer snickers and less laughter occur as the reality of this question sinks in. My final statement to the audience is, "If you don't have your life in order, it may be a bit presumptuous to be telling others how they should be living theirs. Yet, that is exactly what praise tries to do."

At this point a few stammering "Buts" are heard as in "But, but, but…" Then I ask someone to clarify, and I am informed that when they praise someone (child, spouse, friend, employee), they really are only doing it for that someone's own good! Perhaps. Perhaps not. I read somewhere that "Good intentions can, at times, pave the road to h---." But what really happens following this audience statement is that the hair on the back of my neck begins to stand straight out just like I have received a strong dose of static electricity. Then I ask the audience "How do you know what is best for me when you have just admitted that you don't even have your own life completely in order?" At this point (all along, acting a bit on my part) I pretend that I am an attorney who has just finished a cross examination of a damaging witness. I turn away, in disgust, and walk away muttering so that the jury can hear me, "How about let's wait until you have your life in order, then you can come and tell me how to live mine!"

A point to ponder within this caution for praise is that often parents, especially, will use praise as a tool to try and shape or condition (e.g., Skinnerian behaviorist terms) a child with the goal of making (modifying) the child more like the parents. If this is the goal of the parents, making little Johnny or Suzie more and more like them, they are going to be sadly disappointed. In fact, the only guaranteed way to make children carbon copies of their parents (i.e., hold the same beliefs, etc.), is NOT to manipulate, shape or condition their behavior but, instead, to modify your own behavior and beliefs to be more like theirs! You can become more like them, but it is next to impossible to make them become just like you.

As I mentioned at the beginning of this book, you do not have to accept all that I have to say regarding each of the praise cautions. But stay as opened-minded as you can for possibly accepting bits and pieces, here and there, of my argument and evidence which, cumulatively, may make a convincing case for praising less and encouraging more. As a prompt for you to consider the impact of each praise caution, I will conclude each one with the following question. Answer honestly – no one is watching or listening.

On a scale of 0% to 100%, how persuasive was this caution in impacting your decision regarding your continued use of praise?

2nd *caution*!

Praise: It can be a sneaky way to flatter!

Flattery is like chewing gum. Enjoy it but don't swallow it.
–Hank Ketcham

One may define flattery as that which is most advantageous to the flatter.
–Theophrastus

Flatter me, and I may not believe you. Criticize me, and I may not like you…. Encourage me, and I will not forget you….
–William Arthur Ward

Flattery is the chief tool of all confidence men.
–Napoleon Hill

We all know the saying, "Flattery will get you everywhere!" Flattery is a form of adulation, it often deceives, and it can foster mistrust. Is this the path you want to take in interacting with others? If I, as your editor, exclaimed, "You are just the perfect person to cover such and such news story," would you take my words at face value or would you wonder why, perhaps, you feel like you are experiencing flattery? I suppose it would depend upon the history you have shared with that editor. Young people, often lacking any history with those trying to manipulate them, may simply take a person's flattery comments at face value.

The quotation by Theophrastus, that flattery most benefits the flatterer, supports the fact that praise used to flatter someone is actually a tactic to manipulate that someone – most often to the benefit of the flatterer. And, according to Hill, flattery works best when the receiver is unaware that he or she is being conned. Delivering encouragement carries no such deception.

Flattery can be defined as excessive and insincere praise. Insincere anything is just that – insincere. It is argued that those who most thirst for flattery end up being most negatively impacted by it. The naïve, the needy and the most impressionable are the most vulnerable to flattery, too often confusing it for legitimate praise.

At first, delivered flattery seems great to receive. But, after thinking more about the possible intentions of the deliverer, one may begin to doubt its sincerity. Praise too often is a "buttering up" flattery tool that is used to get something from a person rather than an expression of our valuing that person. In hindsight, it is an empty message.

Another problem with flattery, e.g., excessive praise, is that this time you were positively evaluated – hence, you received flattery. But, if you think about it, for someone to flatter you it implies that they hold a position that allows them to do so. Therefore, it must also be assumed that that flatterer could just as easily, using his or her position, evaluate you negatively. Be on guard!

On a scale of 0% to 100%, how persuasive was this caution in impacting your decision regarding your continued use of praise?

3rd *caution!*

Praise: its most threatening aspect is a need to remain praiseworthy!

Here is my story. While working as a professor at a major university, I often was called upon to Chair various campus committees. I loved every aspect of my job – teaching and advising young people, researching subjects of interest to me, and mingling with colleagues at professional conferences. The one aspect of my job that I disliked (I mean hated) was committee work – especially chairing a committee.

At the start of the school year, I would receive a praising phone call from my Dean. It would go something like this, "Bob, you did such a great job last year chairing "such and such" committee, how about doing it again this year?" You will note that there is more than a hint of "flattery" that was discussed in Caution #2.

Part way through the call I was ready to either hang up or, at least, upchuck. What was I to do? I knew and he knew that his praise of me was a "set up" to get me to agree to undertake the chairperson task this year. Remember what was said at the start of this book - it doesn't matter what my Dean intended his praise message to be (it could well have been sincere praise with no ulterior motive behind his words), it only matters how the receiver (me) interpreted his message. I interpreted his praise as his way to manipulate me into saying "Yes."

Being someone who tries to be a team player, someone who tries to respond when others ask for help, I did, in fact, say "Yes." I knew I was being conditioned. I knew I was being shaped. And, I knew I was being manipulated, but I went along with his request and agreed.

The problem here is that my definition of being praiseworthy may not be the same definition others have for me being praiseworthy. When praised (a sneaky request for chairperson service), I felt an obligation to respond positively. I felt a certain weight on my shoulders. I didn't ask for this weight; I didn't want this weight, but there it was weighing me down. And, because I do not like to let others, including my Dean, down, I let the weight dictate my response to his phone call. I went ahead and assumed the chairmanship of the committee! I suppose I wanted to remain praiseworthy in my Dean's eyes.

Who most benefits from praise? At first glance it may seem that the receiver of praise most benefits. But look a little deeper. My Dean benefited more from his delivered praise than did I. He shaped my behavior – I said "Yes." Next year I suppose that once again I will acquiesce to his request. To make matters even worse, I will probably say "Thank you" implying that I see it as an honor to be asked to chair the committee!

Take another situation where a parent praises a child who uses the "big boy's potty" for the first time. "Great job," "I'm so proud of you," "Just wait until we tell your dad!" Yes, the little boy is being praised. Yes, he likes the positive attention. But the parent wants something in return. The parent wants the child's use of potty behavior to continue. Why? Do I really have to answer this question? Changing stinky diapers simply is not a pleasant thing to do no matter how much you might love the little one. The parameters become immediately obvious to the little boy – continue using the big boy's potty and you will continue being praised. Using the potty, apparently, makes you more praiseworthy in the eyes of the parent.

Children, especially, do not have a fully developed sense of "self." They develop that "self" through, among other things, the messages sent to them by important people in their lives. Should a parent or teacher describe a child's work as "clever," phenomenal," "awesome," "breathtaking," "superb," or dynamite," clearly such messages of evaluation, at first, would be welcomed. But, and there is a "but." These words of praise have raised the bar so high that it is unlikely that the child will be able to maintain such performance. When one is sitting on the top of the mountain, even for a short while, there is only one way go – down.

You can never raise the bar too high by delivering encouragement.

On a scale of 0% to 100%, how persuasive was this caution in impacting your decision regarding your continued use of praise?

4th *caution!*

Praise: It increases, not decreases, the psychological distance between two people!

"You did a great job on that project!" and "I'm very proud of you." For the first statement, who most likely is delivering it – an employee or a boss? For the second statement, who most likely is delivering it – a parent or a child? Your author is not a betting man, but he would bet the first statement, "You did a great job on that project!" was delivered by the boss, not the employee. Your author would also bet that the second statement, "I'm very proud of you," was delivered by a parent not a child. How did he arrive at this conclusion? Probably the same way that you did. You recognized that the unwritten rules of game are, bosses praise employees, not the other way around, and parents praise children, not the other way around.

When one person praises another person, it sends a signal loud and clear that that person holds a higher position or status that allows him or her to dispense praise. As a boss, it goes with the territory, the right, maybe even the responsibility, to praise employees. It is a way of shaping, modifying, or dare I say it, manipulating, employees' behavior. If the employees perform as the boss desires, they will likely receive praise. If they don't perform as desired by the boss, they may either be punished or may not receive expected praise, a form of punishment in and of itself.

This same difference in power scenario exists in a parent / child relationship. The parent holds the superior high ground, carrying with it the right to dispense praise. Report card performance can be praised, success in a sport can be praised, helping with household chores can be praised – all *if* the parent feels it is warranted.

Let's examine another, at first strange sounding, scenario. Let's envision the employee praising the boss; let's envision the child praising the parent. Why does this sound so strange? Well, in the grand pecking order of handing out the behaviorist tool of praise, bosses are ranked higher than employees, and parents are ranked higher than children – with all the rights that accompany that higher ranking or status including dispensing praise.

An internet search asking, "What is it called when employees praise bosses," yielded little. Things that describe a perfect boss were highlighted, but little if anything offered advice on how an employee could praise his or her boss.

Note that when an employee praises a boss, it most often is seen as a form of brown-nosing. More likely, employees praising bosses simply is not seen at all. The same holds true in the home. It is unlikely for children to praise parents. In fact, it is so unlikely that I am not sure, like the brown-nosing term in the workplace, that there is even a term for it.

The bottom line is that the moment one person praises another person, it is at that moment that a psychological distance between the two parties is demonstrated for all the world to see. Praising, a tool most often reserved for use by a more powerful person in a relationship (i.e., boss, parent), increases, not decreases, the psychological distance between two people. This distance is not a horizontal one suggesting equalness between the two parties. Praise is a message between people who are unequal! Praise is a vertical distance suggesting that one party is either above or below the other in power.

On a scale of 0% to 100%, how persuasive was this caution in impacting your decision regarding your continued use of praise?

5th *caution!*

Praise: Must be "handled," sometimes even "denied!"

If praise is so great, if praise is so welcomed by receivers of it, why do so many people seem to react defensively when they receive it? Receivers of praise often treat the praise as if they have just been handed a steaming hot baked potato still wrapped in aluminum foil – it is so hot that it must be "juggled." Don't believe it? Try a little experiment. Select several people and shift into your best praise delivering mode. For the purpose of this exercise, lay it on a bit! Listen for their common defensive responses such as "Gee, anyone could have done it," "It really wasn't that big of a deal," "Oh, I should have used a different stain," and "Here, look at all the mistakes." It is the odd person who simply responds by saying, "Thank you."

Your author's wife, Cecelia, is a case in point. She is a confident and competent professional lady who, as a hobby, can quilt with the very best of them When each quilt that she completes is handed to the lucky recipient (daughter, daughter-in-law, valued neighbor) as a gift and that person praises her for its beauty and craftsmanship, she *immediately* offers denial statements – "You can see where the quilting was not perfectly aligned" or "You should see how much better my fellow quilters have done this same quilt."

Most recently, my wife has been buying long sleeved men's shirts from the Thrift Store and making beautiful aprons with accompanying matching wine bottle carriers made from the shirts' sleeves. Very creative, very eye-catching, and very much appreciated by those lucky enough to receive one of them, but, still, most often the heaped-on praise is denied or at least "juggled" a bit.

By the way, your author is equally guilty of shifting into denial when being praised. A couple years ago he "remodeled" the inside of a used Roadtrek Class B camper van making it better able to accommodate his 6-foot 2-inch height. All his friends and family delivered "Wows," "Gee, I could never have done that," and "You ought to go into business converting vans" statements. You should have seen me in action – I was the champion denier of the praise.

Our reception to praise is a reflection to our self-esteem and feelings of self-worth. Receiving praise often conflicts with our own self-views. Further, some people simply hate being the center of attention with the scary component of evaluation being displayed for all to see. Some people just find it plain embarrassing.

Maybe it is just human nature to deny praise. Perhaps humans have decided that it is better to point out all the mistakes oneself *before* others point them out to you. Who knows? Have you had some of these very same "denial of praise" experiences?

On a scale of 0% to 100%, how persuasive was this caution in impacting your decision regarding your continued use of praise?

6th *caution!*

Praise: It elicits unwanted psychological reactions!

Caution #4, above, often prompts one to *orally* handle bestowed-upon-praise. Caution #5, on the other hand, can elicit unwanted psychological reactions where one's body, not one's words, gives away the discomfort felt when being praised. For instance, blushing is a universal human response to receiving social attention, and what could be a clearer example of such attention than being praised?

How is this discomfort displayed? What is clear is that any discomfort felt by the person being praised is *not* by choice. It is physiological. It just happens! And, when it happens, it can be a bit unsettling to realize just how easy it is for the deliverer of praise to trigger these unwanted reactions.

What kind of reactions are we talking about? To find out for yourself, try a little exercise. Select someone and heap, I mean "heap," on praise. It could be about an outfit the person is wearing, his or her recently baked cinnamon buns, a just finished quilt, a watercolor that won an award, or a high score received on a recent test. Anything will do as a target for the praise.

Lay on the praise and stand back and watch the show! Watch the person's cheeks begin to blush. Note the person's clammy hands. Look for signs of an increased heartbeat. It is worth noting that the person receiving the praise did *not choose* to blush, to have clammy hands, or to exhibit an increased heartbeat. It just happened. The person's body gave his or her discomfort away. It announced loud and clear he felt discomfort. These involuntary reactions can be unsettling.

To take this discussion further, let's "run" another experiment. Let's take two people, called Subject #1 and Subject #2, and place them in two separate soundproof rooms. We then will "wire them up" with sensors to measure the degree of blushing experienced, the clamminess of their hands, and their heart rate. We will run leads from these sensors to gauges located in a third room. A researcher, sitting in this third room, blind to the real purpose of the experiment, will watch the gauges for any signs of change. The experiment continues whereby, at random, one of the Subjects will be "highly praised" and the other Subject will be "verbally punished." The question is, can the researcher in the third room tell from simply reading the gauges, which Subject is being praised and which Subject is being punished?

The answer is "No!" Your body sends out the same signals (increased blushing, clamminess, and heartbeat) whether you are being highly praised or highly verbally punished. Why? It is simple. Both praise and punishment are an evaluation, and most people are uncomfortable being evaluated. Their body reacts accordingly.

On a scale of 0% to 100%, how persuasive was this caution in impacting your decision regarding your continued use of praise?

th *caution!*

Praise: Said to one's face versus overheard praise!

When an audience is asked, "Which type of praise do you most believe, praise said to your face or praise about you that you just happen to overhear?" The answer is unanimous – overheard praise wins the day. When asked "why," respondents say that praise that you happen to overhear must be sincere because the deliverer of the praise could not possibly have any ulterior motive. What is the lesson here? I suppose if you were a die-hard carrot-and-stick behaviorist, you might use this caution to your advantage. But how?

Years ago, early in your author's career, he taught junior high mathematics. At lunch time he had "hall duty" just outside of his classroom door. He shared this student monitoring responsibility with Hazel Beattie, the teacher who had the room next door. She taught English. What we would do is prepare a brief scenario whereby we would plan to "talk about" a selected student, let's say Suzie, at the precise moment that she walked by us on her way to lunch. Our "talk," really just a snippet of a "talk," included saying praiseworthy things about her. "Yep, Suzie really seems to have a real grasp of math," or "It was amazing, Suzie was the only one who seemed to understand the author's point."

Even closer to home, at least for your author, were his experiences of riding in the back seat of the car while his mom and dad talked in the front seat. There were no seat belts then so on any ride of any length I would lie sideways on the back seat and often "pretend" to fall asleep. I thought that I had my parents fooled. Little Bobby was fast asleep. What happened next was that at just that moment my dad, especially, would start saying praiseworthy things about me. There I lay, smiling from ear to ear as I absorbed their praise about me. And, of course, the praise all must be true because they couldn't know that I was wide awake and listening. On hindsight, I never realized how crafty, perhaps a bit sneaky, my parents were.

Examine your own life. Where do you recall "overhearing" praise about you? Were you smiling from ear to ear, too? Did you think to yourself, "Gee, this must really be what this person or persons think about you." Moving on, where do you recall having used the same delivering overheard praise on others. Did you catch them smiling from ear to ear?

Now, it appears that if praise, even overheard praise, is sincere, then what is the problem? Well, for earlier mentioned cautions (i.e., designed to manipulate), even sincere praise can manipulate. The real question here is WHY is overheard praise so believable? Why can't we simply praise someone to his face? Unfortunately, we have all learned to be gun-shy of such praise, believing that it only is being delivered to direct, shape, or manipulate us.

Jumping ahead to later in this book, it should be noted that you can deliver encouragement face to face without any of the suspicions associated with face to face delivered praise.

On a scale of 0% to 100%, how persuasive was this caution in impacting your decision regarding your continued use of praise?

8th *caution!*

Praise: It can "use" a child or other person for an ulterior motive!

> *Never praise through comparison.*
> Katerina Mery

No one likes to be "used." Maybe, even worse, no one likes being used and not knowing one is being used. This is not how we should treat each other. This is a misuse of a superior's power. The problem with praise in this situation is best explained through the following short story.

Becky's Story

A preschool teacher moves around the room *"catching"* children behaving appropriately. She spots Becky sitting quietly at her desk, with her hands folded, giving her eye contact, and seemingly ready to listen. The teacher loads on the praise. She loudly announces, "I really like the way Becky is sitting so nice and quiet and ready to work." You might ask, "What could possibly be wrong here?"

- The teacher has not done Becky any favors. Just wait until playground time when she likely will be razzed by fellow students. *"Hey, there goes Miss 'nice and quiet' dork Becky."*

- The teacher is *pretending* to speak to Becky, but she is just "using" her to manipulate (control) the behavior of all the other children in the classroom. This is simply not a nice way to deal with human beings. It also is a bit sneaky, isn't it?

- The teacher has just introduced *competition* into the situation. Now everyone is in a *contest* to see who can be the nicest, quietest, student – just what the teacher wanted in the first place. Isn't there a better reason for "being ready to learn" that benefits all students?

- The teacher's statement, "I like…." stresses that the reason for *"being quiet and ready to work"* has more to do with keeping the teacher happy than in how such behavior can contribute to a positive learning environment within the classroom. Students are not there to serve a teacher's "I like" this or that.

Let's move beyond Becky's preschool example. Review your own family, for instance, of where you have used these same techniques. Have you praised one of your children in earshot of a sibling in hopes that by praising one child you could have an impact on the others? Have you been in a work situation where these same tactics were used on you?

Another example of the connection between receiving praise and being compared to others takes place when potential deliverers of praise (parents, teachers, coaches, or managers) tell those seeking praise, "Just go in there and give it your best," "Give it your all, give it the good old college try." Let's assume that the person desiring praise does just that – gives it his all. Afterall, how much better can one do than give it his best or give it his all? The problem is that his receiving praise depends more upon the performance of others than it does his own performance. Encouragement does not pit one person's performance against another's.

Your author has spent a good bit of time observing Montessori children in their learning environment. One might have 25 kids doing 25 different activities, each intent upon doing their selected activity to the best of their ability, without looking over their shoulder at how other students are doing. It is eye-opening to watch how driven the kids seem to be without any promise of praise other than the "internal" self-praise that comes from mastering a task. And don't for a moment think that Montessori students do not compete! The do. They compete with enthusiasm, determination, and focus, BUT they compete with their own prior performance not with the performance of classmates. Visit a nearby Montessori School and observe this for yourself.

On a scale of 0% to 100%, how persuasive was this caution in impacting your decision regarding your continued use of praise?

9th *caution!*

Praise: Sandwich effect, "You did a great job, *but…!*"

Negative feedback is never easy to give, but sandwiching criticism between layers of praise makes it more palatable and more effective.
–Anne Dohrenwend

The feedback sandwich is a product of a lazy, automated approach to management.
–Russell Weigandt

A powerful quotation by Richard Steele says it all. "I know of no manner of speaking so offensive as that of giving praise and closing with an exception." You are encouraged to think twice before delivering praise and then ending with a "BUT." I am sure that you think at least twice when you are the recipient of the dreaded "BUT!"

Yet, Mary Kay Way, founder of Mary Kay Cosmetics, believes that praise in one of the most powerful things a leader can offer and, thus, advises her managers to sandwich any feedback criticism remarks between healthy layers of praise. So? Who is right, Richard Steele or Mary Kay?

A review of the literature reveals a surprising large number of "sandwich effect" citations. Some authors call the sandwich effect the "feedback sandwich." Still others, a bit more jaded, call it the "sh.. sandwich." Some even dictate the thickness of the criticism in the middle as compared to the top and bottom delivered praise – i.e., a 3:1 ratio, a 5:1 ratio, or even a 10:1 ration. This, of course, would require a good bit of bookkeeping on the praise deliverer's part.

If I had a nickel for all the "BUTs" that have followed praise that I have received in my life, I would be rich. This caution is mirrored in the ideas presented in the famous little book, *The One Minute Manager*, authored by K. Blanchard and S. Johnson (1982). The authors tell us to use one minute reinforcing our company or institution goals, one-minute praising, and one-minute reprimands. You know and I know that when step two, the one-minute praising, is happening, the only thing that you are thinking about as an employee, student or child is the about to be delivered, step three, one minute of reprimands. These reprimands are the real BUT of the message. Perhaps I should have said, these reprimands are the real "BUTT" of the message!

Another three-step approach goes something like this. As a boss, parent, or teacher, approaches the employee, child, or student, the superior should:

1) Tell the person what a great job he or she is doing (be sure to smile).

2) Drop the BUT (i.e., criticism) on him or her – the real reason for your behaviorist shaping message.

3) Exit quickly saying over your shoulder, "Keep up the good work."

Ask yourself, which of the recommended three steps in *The One Minute Manager* will you most remember? Probably the reprimands. Which of the alternate three step approach, above, will you most likely remember? Surely it will be the BUT message.

The sandwich effect can be seen as a bit like delivering a sucker punch. The experienced boxer feigns a punch with his right hand only to deliver the real punch, the equivalent of the sandwich criticism punch, to his opponent's gut. The opponent never saw the real punch coming until it was too late.

Authors who favor the praise sandwich go on to describe how important it is to deliver it effectively. What does this mean? Deliver your message with a dramatic force, using all of the skills actors use to engage and inform their audiences – increased or decreased volume, a rise in inflection, and a pregnant pause mixed in with a bit of humor is recommended.

No matter how well the feedback sandwich is delivered, children, and others, quickly get tuned in to the praise-criticism-praise pattern and, therefore, ignore the praise because it is just a lead-in to the criticism.

On a scale of 0% to 100%, how persuasive was this caution in impacting your decision regarding your continued use of praise?

10th *caution!*

Praise: Delivered as a pronouncement of a guaranteed future event!

Conjure up a picture or scenario where a student has a big test coming up, a high school senior has his fingers crossed in hopes of being accepted to the college of her choice, or the young athlete is about to compete for the coveted county trophy. These scenarios are not just limited to kids. It could be that a man or woman who is applying for a job promotion, someone who hopes that his book will be accepted by a publisher, or a young couple that hopes and prays that the latest round of in vitro insemination will be successful.

What might be a possible downside, as caring parents, friends, family members, colleagues, coaches, and teachers, to delivering praise-oriented messages that offer some sort of future prognostication?

Here are some examples of such well-meaning, but possibly unhelpful, (even hurtful, praise-oriented) messages.

"How is my going-to-ace-the-test student doing?"

"Your dad and I just know that you are a "shoe-in" to get accepted. No doubt about it!"

"We are sure that you will be bringing home the "gold" and doing our school proud!"

"You are clearly the best qualified person to get that promotion. We all know that!"

"I think your book was great. I am sure that many publishers will recognize its greatness!"

"We know this time around everything will work out. You are going to make great parents!"

What happens when the test is not aced, the sought-after college acceptance is not offered, or the county trophy is not brought home? What happens when someone else gets that promotion, the book manuscript is turned down, or the in vitro insemination procedure was not successful. In addition to personally having to deal with the feelings of the not acing the test, the college turn down, the unachieved county trophy, the denied promotion, the back-tosquare-one feeling regarding the book manuscript, and the failed medical procedure, one now has the added weight of having let down those who were rooting for him or her!

Logically, we all know that the odds are that not all students are going to ace the test, not all college applicants will be successful getting accepted to the college of their choice, not all sought job promotions will be secured, and not all tournaments will end with everyone being the winner. In fact, using the playoffs in basketball as an example, we have eight teams from each conference (East and West). So, the odds are that only 1 in 16 will be the winner. The other teams (and players) will have to personally handle their loss, as well as handle facing any and all supporters and fans who "Just knew they were going to bring home the gold!"

For adults, this kind of pressure might be acceptable. But to dump this kind of pressure, this kind of heightened often unrealistic expectations on children, is cruel, especially when supporters could be delivering encouragement messages instead!

The following short story, a real story at that, reveals how what were probably well-intentioned words of support were, in the listener's ears, just the opposite.

Nicole's Story

Hi Dr. Tauber

I was unlucky enough to experience some of the negative effects of praise during a conversation with my new principal who recently hired me. She told me how she just "knows that I am going to do a wonderful job as a teacher," and believes that I am going to be a great asset to the school. All I know was that I have never felt so sick in my life! The more she kept telling me that she had faith in my abilities, the more I just wanted her to shut up!

Now I feel SO much pressure is being placed on my shoulders. In fact, just in writing this email I am getting nauseous thinking about my job. It wasn't bad enough that I put pressure on myself, now I feel that I risk letting my principal down if I don't live up to her expectations. This really is a terrible feeling.

Regards,

Nicole

On a scale of 0% to 100%, how persuasive was this caution in impacting your decision regarding your continued use of praise?

11th *caution!*

Praise: It feels good receiving it, but often feels punishing when one is expecting it and does not get it!

There is no arguing that being praised feels good. It feels even better if one is ignorant, a form of bliss in itself, of the cautions for delivering praise in the first place. But we know that we are not always praiseworthy. We know that even if we were always praiseworthy, it is unlikely that those in a position to praise us would always be around to catch us being praiseworthy. Hence, even in ideal conditions there will be times when we expected to be praised, but we did not receive it. This can hurt. Was it an oversight or was it intended – that is the question.

No one has addressed this feature of expecting praise and not receiving it more thoroughly than Alfie Kohn, the author of *Punished by Rewards: The Trouble with Gold Stars, Incentive Plans, A's, Praise, and Other Bribes*. His book clearly is a challenge to the carrot-and-stick psychology practiced in many homes, schools, and work environs. The underlying theme to this approach is "do this and you will get that." Unfortunately, in our busy world today, there are simply not enough praise dispensers (reminds me of a candy PEZ Dispenser) to hand out the expected coveted praise to all those deemed worthy.

Unless one lives and dies by the carrot-and-stick approach to parenting, teaching, and managing, one might consider teaching kids, students, and employees what quality looks like so that they can recognize it when they achieve it, and then help themselves to praise and rewards. The difference, here, is that the child, student, or employee is more the CEO (Chief Executive Officer) of his own life – a skill and attitude that will serve him or her well in adulthood.

An ongoing experiment conducted by your author consisted of decorating a small Styrofoam cooler to look like a pirate's treasure chest. It then was filled to the top with all sorts of trinkets – stickers, pencils, frig magnets – most contributed for free from local stores. The chest was set in the corner of a 2nd grade classroom and the students were told "If you think that you have done quality work, then feel free to help yourself to a reward" (e.g., tangible praise). Of course, the students were taught what "quality work" looked like so that they could make an informed decision.

What happened? At first there was a bit of a run on the pirate chest rewards. Then it quickly tapered off. By the second week students began to make quality decisions about their quality work, seeking a reward only if they felt that they really "deserved it." Soon, most students weaned themselves from even needing an external reward, instead relying on an internal reward for a job well done! They praised themselves! The point is that they made these grown-up decisions on their own. They became their own CEO.

A Montessori Student Being His Own CEO

The story goes like this. While visiting a Montessori School, I was talking with the Directress, and observed 25 children (age 6 - 9), each with a clear sense of purpose, working on 25 different projects. This was amazing to watch. No one seemed to be looking over his or her shoulder to see if the Directress was watching, hence, hoping to later receive praise from her. They worked, and "work" it was in their mind, trying to achieve as best they could without being influenced by how well a neighboring child was doing on his or her project.

But what really surprised me was that halfway through my observation, one boy walked to the center of the room, picked up a bell, and rang it. Everyone in the room turned to see the source of, and reason for, the bell ringing. At that moment Jason, the bell ringer, announced with great pride that he has successfully completed the Trinomial Cube, an abstract math concept precursor to algebra. All the students clapped, a form of praise for him. What was the difference between his situation and other situations where the adult (parent, teacher, boss) is the only one designated to announce praiseworthy events? Here, Jason had been taught quality, recognized quality, persisted in successfully completing the Cube, and decided (note, *he* decided) that his accomplishment was worthy of praise!

On a personal level your author experienced the negative effects of having been praised one year but not the following year. As the story goes, I won the Excellence in Research Award for the year at my college. I received a wall plaque, got my name entered into the "winner" records for that year for that category, and was asked to deliver a speech to my colleagues.

Given that only one of these awards was given each year, the net effect was that we had one winner (me) and almost 200 losers (my colleagues). Needless to say, the congratulatory comments (mostly brief) and handshakes were lukewarm, at best. This story relates to this praise caution in that for the following year, apparently my research output / quality no longer "measured up." How do I know? Well, I was not selected for the award that year even though I thought I had a good chance at winning. It felt punishing. Now it was my turn to be among the almost 200 losers.

On a scale of 0% to 100%, how persuasive was this caution in impacting your decision regarding your continued use of praise?

12th *caution!*

Praise: It can be addictive - as an end in and of itself. Kids can, in effect, get "hooked on praise!"

Lots of things can become a habit – things you can't live without. We can get hooked on them. They can become an addiction controlling our life's decisions. For some, the debilitating habit could be drugs, alcohol, or cigarettes. Most people understand how these addictions can be damaging. But there is another addiction that can be damaging, especially for children. That is being "hooked" on praise. They can become praise junkies.

There is a cynical tongue-in-cheek twist to the statement, "Be sure you are being noticed when you do a good dead! Otherwise, what's the point?" One would hope that we would do good deeds just for the sake of doing them and not for the acclaim or merit badges that might accompany such behavior if noticed. Apparently, society teaches us otherwise, and children, keen observers of their peer and adult role models, catch on fast.

If I don't receive a reward or praise for doing something, then that something, apparently, must not be worth doing. There is a picture that I wish I could show you, but I will have to simply describe it. Imagine an elementary school teacher who, herself, seems hooked on praise and rewards and, in turn, uses them to impact student behaviors. The picture is one of a little girl in class who has many, many praise stickers (i.e., Great Job," "Tremendous," "You are the Best,") and several "1st place" ribbons plastered all over her face. It is surprising that she can still see or breathe.

My daughter, when in 2nd grade, brought home a worksheet where the teacher had handwritten in bold red marker, "Great Job," had written a large "A+ on it, and even affixed a scratch-and-sniff sticker of a cucumber, yes, a cucumber, to the sheet. The teacher, apparently, was hooked on praise and seemed to be doing her very best to "hook" her students on it, too.

When a child at home wants to know when asked to take out the trash or to set the table, "What's in it for me?" perhaps the addiction is starting. Children hooked on praise require praise in regular, and sometimes increasing, doses in order to feel validated. The reason praise works, especially in the beginning, is that children are hungry for approval – from parents, teachers, coaches, etc. We can feed their need for external approval, or we can teach them to seek their own approval. Praising children, or for that matter, adults, can make them dependent on that praise even to the extent that they will do anything to get it. Do you want to feed this habit?

On a scale of 0% to 100%, how persuasive was this caution in impacting your decision regarding your continued use of praise?

13th *caution!*

Praise: It can stifle risk-taking in order to continue to remain praiseworthy in the eyes of others!

When someone is praised (i.e., rewarded) for doing something one way, that person is more likely to do it that way in the future. This is the basis of Skinner's operant conditioning. Reward (i.e., praise) someone when you judge their behavior to be worth rewarding, and it is likely that they will repeat that behavior in the future in hopes of again receiving a reward.

Take the lowly experience of "lab rats" who spend their days running mazes. With the rat a bit hungry, food is placed somewhere in the maze toward the rear. The rat then, using any senses available to him, goes in search of the food. The food is his reward. But, when successful, the rat has also "learned." In future maze runs he is more likely to follow the same path that he followed that resulted in finding the food. There may be a better path to take, there may be a shorter path to take, but the rat has learned from experience, via operant learning, via behavior modification, that the initial successful path is the one to follow in the future.

Risk-taking on the part of the rat is avoided. Why take a chance on taking an unproven path when the proven one has been shown to be successful? Rats don't take this opportunity to "think outside of the box" for a better solution to the securing food problem. They don't take this opportunity to examine perhaps more creative solutions. They could, but they don't.

When we leave the rat world and return to the human world, we often find the same "horse-with-blinders-on" approach by those who have been praised. The horse only sees directly ahead of him and that is where he goes unless external pressure from the reigns is felt. The child, having just been praised for demonstrating a specific behavior, tends to repeat that behavior – the same behavior that earned him or her the praise in the first place. His or her behavior is well on its way to being modified or shaped.

The problem is that humans, with their built-in capacity at solving problems, severely limit themselves if they simply repeat the same behaviors and thoughts over and over. New problems often demand creative solutions. They demand a "What if we…." Or "Perhaps we could…." approach. They demand the confidence to try the untried even if that effort does not always earn them praise. Pursuing such untrodden paths demands a passion that transcends the need for external praise. In fact, often it is the journey, itself, towards solving a problem that is more self-rewarding than any external reward or praise that could be offered.

Children who are praised, in many cases, can become afraid to attempt new things. They become afraid of failure. The safest way to avoid failure is to stick to easier challenges and to familiar challenges that are likely to result in success and, thus, bestowed praise! Pursuing greater challenges, on the other hand, offers no such guarantees.

On a scale of 0% to 100%, how persuasive was this caution in impacting your decision regarding your continued use of praise?

14th *caution!*

Praise: It is a relatively scarce commodity. After all, just how many "gold," "silver" and "bronze" stars or "winner" ribbons can we award?

I didn't make it that way, I simply found it that way. Praise, in any and all forms, is a relatively scarce commodity. There is not enough of it to go around. To be honest, we probably do not want to have enough to go around. If everybody was labeled praiseworthy, then nobody would stand out as being praiseworthy. Praiseworthy depends upon some people standing out above the rest. So, we sparingly hand it out. To be honest, some people being praiseworthy also means that some people must stand out below the rest.

There is room for only one final winner in a tennis tournament – Nadal? Federer? But not both! Serena Williams? Maria Sharapova? But not both! We can't even make room for two people at the top, let alone have a "pile" of praiseworthy people at the top.

At least in the Olympics we have room for three praiseworthy people – winner of the Gold, winner of the Silver, and winner of the Bronze. Though, really, we only have the most praiseworthy person, the winner of the Gold, and the two runners-up, Silver and Bronze.

On a scale of 0% to 100%, how persuasive was this caution in impacting your decision regarding your continued use of praise?

15th *caution!*

Praise: Musical Chairs is a "rigged" game!

Although in the Special Olympics we seem to have room to bestow praise on all contestants, clearly worthy and seen as giving it their all, the real world only recognizes, i.e., praises, those at the top – the winners. Whether it is a game of Musical Chairs or an exciting Super Bowl or NCAA finals, only one – person or team – will emerge as being praiseworthy. The others, those who lost or failed along the way, are .... You decide how to end this sentence.

What makes matters worse is that not only is praise a scarce commodity, the path to winning it often is rigged! What do I mean? Take the children's (sometimes adult's, too) game, Musical Chairs.

Watch it being played at recess in school, at a children's birthday party, or at an event such as a reception for adults. It can get nasty. In Musical Chairs we don't have "weight" categories – 125, 133, 141, etc. divisions – as we have in wrestling. And, we don't have skill level categories as we have in baseball (farm club players do not compete against major league players). This guarantees some level of fairness.

Yet, in Musical Chairs it is a free-for-all. Big kids, sometimes really big kids, compete with all the other kids – the smaller, the meek, the frail, etc. Boys compete with girls. Older kids compete with younger kids. Stronger and more athletic kids compete with…. Well, you get the message! The fact is that we (the parents, the teachers), the organizers, really know ahead of time who is more likely to win and who is more likely to lose. The game is more than a bit rigged. It is no different in Dodge Ball where the weakest player is guaranteed to be slammed out of the game, first. Some players, most often the same players, will "earn" the praise of being the-last-man-standing, while most others who do not find a seat, one at a time, will be told to "go stand against the wall."

Your author has provided an anonymous Musical Chair Poem for your consideration. Does the poem ring true for any of you?

A Musical Chairs Poem

There is a children's game with music & motion that starts with great promise.
But soon children realize the game is rigged so it is a bit dishonest.

Big kids and small kids, those coordinated, those not,
Are pitted against each other, success for some a long shot.

Where do all the children go when they cannot grab a chair?
They find themselves labeled as "out," and are told to stand over
there!

As the pile of "losers" grows and grows, their fun begins to
diminish.
At least in a game like kickball kids are all involved from start-to-
finish.

More & more children are sidelined, knowing that they should have
fought harder at all cost.
The message they've learned is that their happiness derives from
others' loss.

With every passing moment fewer and fewer kids will be having any
fun.
Their positive self-image, cooperation, and confidence undone.

But if this is what really happens, why do kids continue to play?
Could it be that as children they simply do what adults say?

The final chair grabber is the one who clearly beat them all,
But maybe winning by beating weaker friends is not winning at all!

If this poem gets you thinking, if it takes you back to your game playing childhood where you often were "out" quickly and often, you might want to consider another way of playing Musical Chairs for your own children, for your own students, etc. Believe it or not there is another way of playing Musical Chairs where everyone wins!

The initial setting is the same for both the win-lose and the win-win versions of the game. Let's say we have 10 players, we have 9 chairs, we have music, and we have movement – all the ingredients for a fun day. In the win-lose version, the rules are that the players will listen to the music and march around a circle of chairs getting ready to grab a chair when the music stops. Because there are 10 players and only 9 chairs, someone – a loser – will be left standing and told to move to the side of the room. The game continues, now with 9 players and only 8 chairs. Each time the music stops we have one more player to add to the loser pile. The winner, and as is the case in most games, the surviving player, is the only one deemed praiseworthy.

For your amusement (not really amusing at all)), view the internet YouTube titled, "Happy New Year, Charlie Brown! – Musical Chairs." Sally gets left out. Marcie gets left out. Lucy gets left out. And, with only Peppermint Patty and Charlie Brown remaining, Charlie Brown gets left out! Now you might think, "What's the harm?" The fact is that this game only guarantees enough "praise" for one player – the winner. You might be reminded that no one takes a game of Musical Chairs more seriously than teenagers and adults. Players of all ages have even been injured to the extent that a hospital visit was warranted. There are some Musical Chairs instances where the person in charge demands waivers to be signed by all players.

In the alternative, win-win, version of playing Musical Chairs everything starts out the same, but the rules are a bit different. This time when the players march around the chairs and the music stops, the goal of the players is to get 10 bums onto the available 9 chairs with their feet clearly off the floor. A chair is then removed. When the music again stops the goal is a bit more difficult. The players need to get those same 10 bums on the remaining 8 chairs with their feet off of the floor. The game really gets challenging, and requires some creative solutions, as more and more chairs are removed.

Players have to work together. Creative solutions are required – put the bigger kids on the bottom and let the smaller kids sit on their laps or, make a "bridge" from one chair to another one using the legs of a bigger player. Note that each time that the music stops in this version of the game we have nothing but winners because all players have been ENCOURAGED to work together to solve their common problem. You might recognize this version of

Musical Chairs as being not all that different from the team building or motivational exercises conducted by major businesses. At this point one might ask, "As organizers of children's games is Musical Chairs played the traditional way the best we can come up with?"

One message that is taught by playing Musical Chairs, with only one person or team being found praiseworthy, is captured by Vince Lombardi's famous quotation, "Winning isn't everything, it's the only thing." He is right. It will be the "only thing" for a select group of people.

On a personal note, I would challenge anyone who says, "But, Dr. Tauber don't children have to learn to lose. They can't just win, win, win – that is unrealistic. The fact is that children today, just like children of yesteryears, experience load and loads of opportunities to lose – a personal illness including anything from a sprained or broken ankle to cancer, an accident, a divorce, a parent losing a job, being mugged in school or on the way to and from school, growing up in a home where education might not be valued, "seeing" drugs being sold on a local street corner, being a stutterer like your author, having a bad complexion in his teens like your author, being unathletic, being a plain Jane, lacking the natural intellect to succeed in math and science, being born on the wrong side of the tracks (where, when young, your author's father broke his neck, whereby he had to move from a nice home into a converted barn with no inside plumbing), and the list goes on and on. No children are immune from loss. Watch your evening newscasts for confirmation of this statement!

If there are so many opportunities for children to experience loss, why then would adults design a game that with 20 players that guarantees 19 of them will lose. The sad part is that if these kinds of games (i.e., musical chairs , dodge ball) are the only games in town to play then, of course, children will play them and select small number of children will win, win, and win, earning praise and more praise. What about the rest of the kids?

On a scale of 0% to 100%, how persuasive was this caution in impacting your decision regarding your continued use of praise?

16th *caution!*

Praise: It can contribute to narcissism!

In Greek mythology, a character named Narcissist saw his reflection in a pool of water and fell in love with it. It reminds me of the 1957 musical, *West Side Story*, where Maria sings, "I feel pretty, Oh, so pretty…And I pity, any girl who isn't me today." Clearly, she feels special, she feels entitled!

Narcissistic people exhibit several symptoms. Among them are "an inflated sense of self-importance," and a "need for excessive attention." Praise, especially lavish and prolonged praise, can be contributors. Encouragement, on the other hand, does not contribute to narcissism. All children, of course, want their parents' approval and attention. Parents can decide the healthiest way to respond to that want. Now that you, as the reader, have read this book, you are aware that you have a choice – supply praise *or* supply encouragement. Choose wisely.

We teach people to be "good losers." Perhaps we should be equally diligent in teaching people to be "good winners." Because praise is something that has power only when sparingly doled out, those talented or lucky enough to receive it may interpret its awarding as something more than it was intended to communicate. Unless the deliverer of the praise meant it to convey a grandiose sense of self-importance, a sense of entitlement, or an excuse for arrogance, these possible byproducts of too much praise can be harmful.

On a scale of 0% to 100%, how persuasive was this caution in impacting your decision regarding your continued use of praise?

17th *caution!*

Praise: It can diminish the value of intrinsic rewards!

Too often well-meaning parents and teachers justify their use of praise by thinking, "I will lay on the praise heavily now in order to motivate (i.e., manipulate or shape) my children to do such-and-such, but, once motivated, I plan to wean them from my delivery of, and their reliance on, praise." Simply put, this does not work.

If you are using praise, you probably feel comfortable with B. F. Skinner's operant conditioning principles whereby supplying a reward (e.g., praise) is a common and major tool to modify or shape another's behavior. What you might not realize is that in using this tool you also are modifying your own behavior! In operant conditioning we tend to continue what works for us, what pays off for us. If you experience success in delivering your praise – you get your children to do what you want them to do – you are likely to continue, not stop or reduce, your use of praise. Your good intentions of later weaning yourself and your children from a dependence on praise goes out the window. By this time, your children are likely to be hooked on receiving praise, and you are likely to be hooked on delivering it. It is hard to give up any "habit" that seems to be working!

The result is that, according to Mark Tyrrell, "excessively praising someone could actually make them less happy in the long run because it can diminish their capacity to find intrinsic reward in anything." Of course, no parent or teacher would purposefully set out to squelch a child's intrinsic reward, but this is what will likely happen when one is continually evaluated, judged, or assessed via external rewards. The question is, at what point will the child ever experience the sheer joy of doing something or pursuing some goal for its intrinsic, not extrinsic, value?

If you would like to see an environment for children, preschool through high school, that thrives on intrinsic rather than extrinsic rewards, visit a Montessori School. There are no external rewards, no classroom sticker charts with gold, silver and bronze stars awarded by a teacher. Children explore, as individuals or occasionally in small groups, what interests them most at the moment. This works because the Montessori environment is a prepared environment, meaning that everything, and I mean everything, in the environment is didactic – meaning designed to teach.

Your author once supervised student teachers in a traditional classroom where he observed one of his interns teaching first grade. While observing, the children's activities were interrupted at short, regular intervals by the intern playing a few cords on the piano. It looked like musical chairs. When I asked, later, why the constant interruptions, the intern said that her co-operating teacher believed that children have very short attention spans and, therefore, need to change activities often. Otherwise, they lose interest and focus. Yet, in a Montessori School one regularly observes 3-year-olds and up focusing on a task for extended periods of time stopping only at the point when the didactic (designed to teach) task being attempted is completed. The task, itself, provides a built-in indicator of when it has been accurately completed. Completing the task, itself, is a form of intrinsic reward. No adult, parent or teacher is required to provide external, "Great job" or "I am so proud of you" rewards.

You simply must see it to believe it – children living in, thriving in, and achieving in a world devoid of external rewards. Is there any competition? Sure, but it is different kind of competition. It is an internal competition to become the best one can be, not an external competition to see if one can be praised for being better than a classmate!

At his point you may be thinking, "But how will this prepare them for the real world?" The proof is in the pudding. Montessori graduates, too, become doctors, lawyers, and Indian Chiefs, and become plumbers, masons, and cosmetologists. The main difference is that whatever they do, or end up as, they got there by responding to internal more than external forces. Gee, what a healthy way to learn!

I took a break today to go and watch my 10-year-old grandson play soccer. When the game was over, and the players came running to the sidelines where the adults stood, I listened to the first words out of the parents' mouths. The vast majority of them delivered **praise** in some form by saying "You were tremendous," "I am really proud of you," "You deserve an ice cream treat," For those parents who arrived mid-way through the game and didn't know the score, their first words to their child were, "What was the final score?" Almost no one said the simple, **encouraging** words, "Did you have fun today?"

On a scale of 0% to 100%, how persuasive was this caution in impacting your decision regarding your continued use of praise?

18th *caution!*

Praise: False praise can be worse than no praise at all!

Praise often is false – or at least it is clear to everyone, including the recipient, that it was ***not*** earned. Take two kids playing softball. One hits a home run and the other strikes out. Both get as rousing exclamation of "Good Job." One student in class quickly masters long division, another clearly struggles with the concept. Both get a "Good Job" from the teacher as she cruises up and down the aisles. But kids are not stupid; they know the truth!

Your "Good Job" takes on far less meaning to the child who did well because he or she realizes that you give this same (or similar) message to everyone. Your "Good Job" to the child who clearly did not do well suggests that either you are lying, you are blind, or you simply do not know how else to respond. I suggest it is the latter – "What should I say?"

Encouragement is not only an acceptable alternative to praise, especially unearned praise, there is no "little white lie" involved. Encouragement can help spur the recipient towards eventually mastering the task at hand. For instance, to the softball player who struck out, one could say, "Ok, we'll (suggesting we are all in this together) "get um "next time at bat." To the student trying to master long division, one could say, "Yeh. When I first tried to do it, it took me forever. I never thought that I would get it." Unfortunately, praise just seems to jump out of our mouths.

It is interesting to note that less capable children are praised more *and* praised for less challenging accomplishments – e.g., dusting erasers, sitting quietly. The adult's praise, in effect, announces to all within earshot, "You are weak, less capable and, thus, in need of praise." It can be very humiliating! It can erode one's self-esteem, just the opposite of what I am sure the praise sender intended.

On a scale of 0% to 100%, how persuasive was this caution in impacting your decision regarding your continued use of praise?

19th *caution!*

Praise: It creates unexpected problems for those trying to stop using it!

Although this caution was partially addressed, earlier, it is worth further mention. "I could stop anytime I want!" – so said my brother about smoking until after 50 years he *finally* stopped cold turkey. So said the drug user hooked on his or her choice of drug. We all like to believe that we, not others, are in control of our own destiny; but when it comes to breaking a long-term habit, I am not so sure.

Many parents have developed the habit of supplying praise to their children, part of what B. F. Skinner would refer to the "carrot" in the carrot-and-the-stick approach. Parents are, in a way, suckered into the use of praise because *it works*, and it particularly worked well when their children were very young, completely dependent upon them for not only the "goodies" in life, but for life, itself.

But then, something seems to happen when the kids reach their teens. What happens can be heard in conversations parents have with each other at a neighborhood party - "My son used to listen to me, but now it seems as if I am just talking to a brick wall!"

The "carrots" that parents depended upon to shape their children's behaviors just don't seem to work any longer.

So, what should parents do? They are used to supplying praise (and other rewards) and they are used to it working. They now have two choices. One, they could increase the intensity, and frequency of their praise believing that praise works, but they just need to up the ante. Or, two, they could decide to abandon praise and try a Plan B – stop praising and start encouraging. Number one is tempting because it is something the parents are used to delivering. Number two can be a bit scary because it means having to abandon what, until recently, seemed to have been working. Just as children (and others) can become "hooked" on receiving praise, parents, too can become "hooked." Breaking the habit, any habit, can be daunting.

Stop spinning your wheels. William Glasser, a renowned psychologist, in his book, *Choice Theory* (1999), tells the reader to try something else if what you are doing is not working – don't just keep doing the same unproductive thing over and over. He is amazed how committed some people are to repeating actions that have not proved fruitful. He describes a person stuck in the snow with his tires beginning to spin. The driver tries to extricate himself by pushing the gas pedal down a little further. What happens – the tires spin more. Undaunted, and convinced that what isn't working now will somehow magically start working, the driver pushes the gas pedal clear to the floor. You know the outcome. The wheels really spin making that "wonderfully" satisfying whine, and the car settles to the frame in the snow and is "stuck." Stop pushing your "praise" peddle to the floor and hoping that "just a little more of it is sure to work."

It is time to stop doing what isn't working or isn't working well. Time to call the *AAA*. Time for a pedagogical Plan "B." It is time to substitute encouragement for praise.

On a scale of 0% to 100%, how persuasive was this caution in impacting your decision regarding your continued use of praise?

20th *caution!*

Praise: Children, especially, might not really expect it nor want it!

It may seem strange, especially to adults who might not find the world so new and wonderous as do children, to hear that children simply like to learn! Unraveling the world, becoming more independent through mastery of skills and knowledge, and doing it all by yourself, are self-motivating. Being praised, on the other hand, may be seen as delivering unwanted attention causing the child to feel embarrassed.

Children (and adults) don't always expect praise. You may be surprised to observe a child working with more persistence when you say or do nothing – but you do it well! You create an environment conducive to learning and discovery, you quietly and unobtrusively observe, and you stay the heck out of the way!

In a Montessori school, students do not expect praise from their director or directress. This works because students are taught what quality looks like in the first place. For instance, building a Montessori "pink tower" or "completing the 1000s chain" can only be done one way. When it is completed as it was taught, students do not require an adult to tell them that they have done it correctly. They can see that for themselves. A personal satisfaction – "I did it! – exists. No external praise is required.

If a child wants feedback from you, she will ask, perhaps in the form of coming to you, showing you her latest creation (i.e., picture, puzzle solved), and excitedly saying, "Look what I did!" This is not the time to take over and bestow bushels of praise. But it is the time to say something. In your mind, play back all the times that your child came and showed you his special something. Edit the tape carefully and you will find that the child did not specifically ask you for praise. What she did do, through her words and very presence standing in front of you, was to solicit some acknowledgement from you. That acknowledgement could be praise or it could be encouragement. You decide.

I am willing to bet that if you provide non-evaluative encouragement, your child will not slink away mumbling, "Where the heck was my praise?"

On a scale of 0% to 100%, how persuasive was this caution in impacting your decision regarding your continued use of praise?

21st *caution!*

Praise: The Person Praising Must be Athletic!

Be careful not to do your good deeds when no one's watching you.
                                        –Tom Lehrer

Take this quotation with a tongue-and-cheek attitude, although the basis of one person praising another person is that the person doing the praising must first observe the person's behavior that may be praiseworthy.

In behavior modification, B. F. Skinner's world, receiving praise is most often assumed to be a reward. In order to shape someone's future behavior (his or her past and present behavior cannot be altered), behaviorists use just four consequences. These include:

- supplying a reward - something you believe a person (or your dog, Fido!) values
- supplying punishment - something you believe a person finds painful,
- supplying time-out - removing something you believe a person values, and
- supplying negative reinforcement - removing something you believe a person finds painful.

It all boils down to an understanding with the other person that, "If you do such and such, then a pleasant or unpleasant consequence will occur." You have control over what consequence that will be. "If you do what I want you to do, then I will supply either positive reinforcement or negative reinforcement." Note the word reinforcement is the critical word, not the word negative. Or I could say, "If you continue doing what I don't want you to do, I will supply either punishment or time-out." Once again, you can decide.

Where does "praise" fit as a consequence? Is it a reward? For some people, yes! For some people, no! If "praise" is something to be valued, then it can either be supplied (acts as a reward) or removed (acts as a time-out). If praise is something to be avoided, then it can be supplied (acts as a punishment) or removed (acts as negative reinforcement). How praise is valued or not valued is totally in the eyes of the beholder, not the supplier.

The dispenser of praise must be in good physical shape, capable of being constantly on the move, and have eyes in the back of his or her head in order to promptly and fairly dispense that praise. Missed praise is useless praise. Why? Because the whole field of contingency management depends upon the consequence, praise in our case, being delivered close enough in time to be associated with the praiseworthy behavior.

Take my dog Ginger. Giving her a desired dog biscuit immediately after she "sits," as commanded, is very different from giving her that same biscuit two hours later. Now, pretend that you have a class of 30 students or a shop floor of employees, all potential receivers of praise if only you can "catch them" engaging in desired behaviors. By the end of the day, even sooner, you likely will be exhausted.

On a scale of 0% to 100%, how persuasive was this caution in impacting your decision regarding your continued use of praise?

SUMMARY OF PRAISE CAUTIONS

1st Praise: Designed to manipulate!
2nd Praise: Can be a sneaky way to flatter!

3rd Praise: Most threatening aspect; remaining praiseworthy!
4th Praise: Increases psychological distance between two people!
5th Praise: Must be "handled," even "denied!"
6th Praise: Can elicit unwanted physiological reactions!
7th Praise: Said to one's face versus overheard praise!
8th Praise: "Uses" another person for an ulterior motive!
9th Praise: Sandwich effect, "You did a great job, but….!"
10th Praise: A pronouncement of a guaranteed future event!
11th Praise: Feels good receiving it; feels punishing if not receiving it!
12th Praise: Can be addictive as an end in itself!
13th Praise: Can stifle passion and risk taking!
14th Praise: It is a relatively scarce commodity!
15th Praise: Musical Chairs is a "rigged" game!
16th Praise: Can contribute to narcissism!
17th Praise: Can diminish the value of intrinsic rewards!
18th Praise: False praise can be worse than no praise at all!
19th Praise: Unexpected problems for those trying to stop!
20th Praise: Children, especially, might not really expect it!
21st Praise: The Person Praising Must be Athletic!

WHAT PERCENT OF EACH CAUTION DO YOU ACCEPT?

You were asked at the conclusion of each of the cautions for using praise to stick your neck out and indicate on a 0% to 100% scale how convincing each caution was. It should have proved interesting to see which cautions offered were the most persuasive. It should also be interesting to see if collectively the cautions have swayed you enough to either stop *OR* significantly reduce using praise and, instead, substitute the use of encouragement.

A FINAL TEST

There is a final test to determine if your message to someone is perceived as praise or as encouragement!

- If your message is perceived as praise, it is likely that any further dialogue between the two of you will cease. After all, what else is there to say when someone utters, "Good job," other than, "Thanks?"

- If your message is perceived as encouragement, it is likely that a dialogue will ensue. Saying, for instance, "Gosh. With so little to go on, how did you ever figure out how to solve that problem?" or "What made you decide to use those three colors together in your quilt?" is almost an invitation to speak. Encouragement invites a continuing dialogue.

CHAPTER 3

"So long as men praise you, you can be sure that you are not yet on
your own true path but on someone else's."
(–Friedrich Nietzsche)

A Preferred Alternative, Encouragement

It would be unfair to offer so many cautions to delivering
praise and then just stop right there. It would be like those people
who complain and complain about things, but who are unwilling or
unable to offer better alternatives. Lots of people believe that they
can see the "problem." Far fewer people can see the solution to the
problem. So as not to be seen as a hypocrite, this chapter is intended
to address the alternative to praise – that being encouragement.

PREACHER JOHN'S STORY

Picture a bright sunny Sunday morning where Preacher
John's sermon is just about to come to an end. Your local breakfast
at your favorite chain restaurant awaits those who do not tarry
because across the county other church goers are planning to make
the same beeline. Father John, as everyone knows, has the choir

continue to sing while he makes his way to the front door and positions himself to shake hands with each parishioner who exits the church. You just know that at this rate you will be late for your coveted breakfast.

As you line up to pass Father John, you can hear parishioners in front of you saying something in the form of "Great sermon," or "Fine job." It is only with offering the obligatory praise and accompanying handshake that one can pass and head for the parking lot. What is the preacher to make of these comments? The preacher knows, and the parishioners know, that not a lot of thought has gone into these short, mostly without substance, praise statements. Father John wonders whether his preaching is making a difference in the parishioners' lives.

How do these statements *energize* or *inspire* him to continue? How do they *fortify* or *galvanize* him? How do they *bolster* or *spur* his continued efforts? The fact is, they don't, because the words highlighted (in italics) in the previous three sentences are outcomes from sending encouragement, not praise.

Just imagine a parishioner saying, when it is his or her turn to shake hands, "Preacher John, I am not sure that I completely agree with all that you presented this morning, but you have caused me to start thinking about the topic. I certainly will mull it over. Thank you!" This would be a statement of encouragement on the parishioner's part, and it only took five seconds to deliver.

At this point you may have to call for some smelling salts to revive Preacher John after he faints in surprise. He is not used to this sort of parishioner response to his sermons. Seriously, though, you have plenty of time, while waiting in line, to compose a statement. You could simply deliver praise, "Great sermon," or you could use this opportunity to deliver encouragement. Which statement do you think would be most *energizing, bolstering*, or *spurring* to the preacher?

When presentations are delivered at conferences, it is common for the audience to clap at the end. Other than being a polite signal that the session has concluded, what does the clapping signify? Not a whole lot. On more than one occasion, depending upon the rapport that I had with the audience, I would say, "Thanks for the applause, but what I really would have appreciated would have been one or more of you telling me that what I presented challenged you to think, really think about the topic. It would be nice to know that our time together had an impact." To tell you the truth, I am thinking, "We could train seals to "clap. I would like a bit more of a response!"

As a case in point, has reading this book made any difference in your thinking regarding the delivery of praise? If it has, let me know. It would *bolster* and *energize* me. If it hasn't, then I suppose I have to work at it a bit more. In either case, I would appreciate encouragement rather than praise.

HOW PRAISE AND ENCOURAGEMENT DIFFER!

Immediately below are comparisons of Praise and Encouragement. A review of these comparisons clearly reveals fundamental differences between the two terms. As highlighted earlier in the book, apples are apples and oranges are oranges. So, too, praise is praise and encouragement is encouragement. They are not synonyms.

- Praise and its synonyms include, to evaluate, judge, review, critique, examine, compare, assess, appraise, classify, rank, score, rate, grade, express a favorable judgment, approval or evaluation, scrutinize, gauge, acclaim, hail, applaud, laud, exalt, extol, and tout.

- Encouragement and its synonyms include, to bolster, buoy, fortify, inspire, impart resolution, help, soothe, cushion, sustain, assist, energize, champion, aid, support, fortify, shore up, restore, hearten, invigorate, enliven, rekindle, stir, commiserate, spur, strengthen, rouse, inflame, boost, galvanize, awaken, embolden, revive, renew, cheer, console, and comfort.

When the going gets tough in any endeavor, which it most surely will, which set of the synonyms for praise or for encouragement should you deliver? Which set of synonyms do you think the other person would most welcome and find most helpful? Finally, which set of synonyms would you appreciate receiving?

With an actual workshop audience, as an exercise, I place all the above synonyms, typed on individual slips of paper for both praise and encouragement, in a plastic cereal bowl. I then display two additional bowls, one labeled PRAISE and one labeled ENCOURAGEMENT. Then I move about the audience asking individual members to reach into the first bowl and select a slip of paper. That person then is asked to read aloud the word, (e.g., bolster, judge, evaluate, or sustain), and decide whether the word, and the action that it implies, best fits in the ENCOURAGEMENT or PRAISE bowl. This exercise helps differentiate between praise and encouragement actions.

- Praise is normally delivered *after* a deemed worthy product or event has occurred.

- Encouragement is normally delivered as part of the *ongoing* process to reach a goal.

Given that most tasks of any worth take time to master, having to wait until the finished product or event has occurred to receive praise does little to help one persevere along the way. This is especially unrealistic for young people. Encouragement, on the other hand, helps people carry on, keep going, and hang in there – all attitudes that contribute to success.

- Praise almost always involves one person *evaluating* another person (sometimes, the dog, Fido, too – cats generally don't really care).

- Encouragement acknowledges that it doesn't matter whether you intended your praise to be an evaluation, if that is how it is perceived by the other person, then it is, in fact, an evaluation!

The decider of whether a delivered message is an evaluation resides in the hands (mind) of the person receiving the message, NOT the person delivering the message. The receiver of the message is the ultimate decision-maker over the meaning and impact of a praise message.

- Praise is a reward for a completed achievement.

- Encouragement is an acknowledgement of effort.

Praise makes the recipient wait until the project, the game, the activity, etc. is completed before he or she can be praised. For some people, especially children, that time lapse between starting and fully completing a project can seem endless. Encouragement, on the other hand, can be given from day-one and can continue to be offered throughout the course of completing a task.

- Praise tells people they've satisfied the demands of others.

- Encouragement helps people evaluate their own performance and feel confident about their own ability.

Whose demands *are* most important to satisfy, yours or someone else's? Whose demands *should* be most important to satisfy, yours or someone else's? Reality reminds us that we are all subject to being evaluated by others, but when and where possible should we not satisfy ourselves first? Let's encourage people to recognize quality performance and then shoot for it. Thomas Jefferson's quotation, "I'm a great believer in luck, and the harder I work the more I have of it," applies here. Encouragement bolstering messages help people stay focused on the task at hand and, even when the going gets tough along the way, have the confidence to continue.

- Praise can be withheld as punishment or cheapened by overuse.

- Encouragement cannot be overused or cheapened.

Deliverers of praise walk a very fine line between denying someone praise who was expecting it, hence creating a feeling of punishment, and saturating that person with so much praise such that its impact is lost.

- Praise often is patronizing. It's talking down as if the praiser holds a superior position.

- Encouragement is a message between equals.

The person doing the praising is recognized as the one, and the only one, holding the power - the power to praise. The assumption is that the person receiving the praise is incapable of recognizing praiseworthy behaviors or outcomes. Encouragement recognizes that although two people might hold different titles (e.g., boss or employee, teacher or student, parent or child), that does not necessarily mean that on a given topic, procedure, belief, or position that they are not equals. Sometimes, even the person holding the lower formal position is the one who, for the moment, is the superior.

- Praise, like diamonds, has value only if there is little of it available.

- Encouragement can, and should, repeatedly be given to all people.

Is everybody praiseworthy? In an ideal world the answer would be "yes." But, whether in sports, academics, or job performance, we have long since learned that praise is handed out sparingly. Encouragement, on the other hand, is a bottomless vessel with an endless supply for all.

ENCOURAGEMENT HAS NO NEGATIVE SIDE-EFFECTS

When a new drug that appears to address your medical situation comes on the market and you hear how amazing it is from television actors (or, sometimes advertised as "not actors"), you are immediately ready to "talk to your doctor" as the ad instructs you to do. The new drug seems to be just what you may need to combat your medical problem. But, at the end of the ad, by law, the side-effects of taking the medicine must be announced. Sometimes there is a lengthy list of side-effects including confusion, fever, painful urination, jaundice, or "could cause death!" At this point you have second (and possible 3rd and 4th) thoughts about considering this drug.

How does this drug education paragraph apply to supplying praise and encouragement? It specifically applies to delivering praise. When praise is delivered, especially lavish and continuous praise, unwelcome side-effects often occur including, among other things, lower risk-taking, lower self-esteem, feelings of entitlement, becoming a junkie (i.e., praise). It is clear at this point, that unlike penicillin, a wonder drug that has generally lived up to its promise, praise is not an equivalent wonder drug for use by parents, teachers, coaches, and bosses. Why? Too many, and often too serious, side-effects exist.

It is not uncommon for any internet search regarding the possible negative effects of praise to come up with this list or that list. For instance, one list titled, *The Seven Deadly Flaws*, generated by D. Pink (2009) from his book, *Drive: The Surprising Truth about What Motivates Us,* found that delivering praise can:

1) extinguish intrinsic motivation
2) diminish performance
3) crush creativity
4) crowd out good behavior
5) encourage cheating, short-cuts, and ethical behavior
6) can become addictive, and
7) foster short-term thinking.

You guessed it! No such list of "deadly flaws" has been found for delivering encouragement.

Supplying encouragement, even supplying large and continuous doses of it, does not come with any "on the medicine bottle" warnings. Encouragement is a tool that works well and has no worrisome side-effects. Encouragement is one of few (and free) truly wonder drugs accomplishing all of what it claims to do.

A LIFE CHANGING EXPERIENCE: THE TONYA DEATER STORY!

Your author, Dr. Tauber, asked a student, Tonya Deater, to work with him by doing some research in the university library. She agreed. The topic of research was "praise versus encouragement." Tonya was asked to visit the university library four times, each time investigating a different aspect of praise and of encouragement.

First visit (Definition): For her first visit she was asked to locate journal and or text references that offered a *definition* of praise and a *definition* of encouragement. Later she returned and handed me a sheet of paper with two columns, labeled Praise and Encouragement, under which she had about an almost equal number of entries. The entries filled about half of each column.

Second visit (Examples): For her second visit she was told to locate journal and or text references that offered *examples* of Praise and *examples* of Encouragement. Once again, she returned and submitted a sheet of paper with two columns, labeled Praise and Encouragement, under which she had about an almost equal number of entries.

Third visit (Positive Instances): For her third visit she was instructed to locate journal and or text references that offered *positive instances* of Praise and *positive instances* of Encouragement. One more time, she returned and handed me a sheet of paper with two columns, labeled Praise and Encouragement, under which she had about an almost equal number (half a page) of entries listing references for *positive instances* of praise and of encouragement. No surprises so far.

Can you guess what her final assignment was? Can you guess what she was asked to research during her fourth visit to the library? Can you guess what was the life changing outcome of this fourth library visit? I would have never guessed it in a million years!

Off Tonya went. After considerable time, much more than the first three visits, she finally appeared at my office doorway and in the meekest voice possible said, "Dr. Tauber, I don't think that I did what you wanted me to do." Then she stepped forward and handed me her fourth piece of paper titled Negative Instances with two columns, one for Praise and one for Encouragement. I could not believe what I saw. The left column, the one for Praise, was totally filled, from the top to the bottom, with citations for the Negative Instances of praise. But, the right column, the one for Encouragement, was completely empty! Not a single Negative Instance of encouragement was cited.

I would never have predicted the outcome of her research. Since then, although your author is not a "betting" man, he has challenged audience after audience with his statement, "I will pay $50.00 to the first person who can locate a legitimate reference pointing out the negative impact of delivering encouragement." To date I have not had to pay up! The reason is obvious, there are no bad impacts of supplying encouragement.

Delivering praise statements is a bit like walking on thin ice – it may support your weight, but at any moment it might just give way and grave consequences could follow. No such danger exists when delivering encouragement statements.

Tonya Deater's research changed my way of thinking, my way of parenting, and my way of trying to be a better spouse, sibling, and neighbor. I now try to "catch myself" when I am about to send praise to someone and question whether I am about to deliver it for their good or for mine. I never would have considered this quandary before reviewing Deater's findings.

My burden is lessened by the fact that there is a great alternative to delivering praise out there sitting and waiting for your use. That alternative is delivering encouragement. The next section of this book addresses this alternative.

A CASE FOR ENCOURAGEMENT

Up until now, you may have thought that praise was the only game in town. To quote the famous Mel Brooks, *Blazing Saddles,* movie "There's a new sheriff in town." Think Cleavon Little as the black sheriff, and Gene Wilder as Waco Kid. The new sheriff in town is "encouragement."

A little recall before we proceed. Remember, praise and encouragement are "not" synonyms! And remember that praising is "not" a way of encouraging! Recall, further, the point-by-point contrast of the two terms offered earlier. Basically, praise is delivered after a deemed worthy product or event has occurred, and encouragement is delivered as part of the ongoing process to reach a goal. Finally, be reminded that praise generally judges, evaluates, and critiques, whereas encouragement bolsters, inspires, sustains, imparts resolution, spurs, and galvanizes.

Encouragement focuses upon the process (effort), not the product (outcome). Because all processes, unlike praise, are continuous, it is possible to continually dispense supportive encouragement. Encouragement focuses on the doer, not the deed. The deed is not complete until it is done (i.e., won the state championship, got accepted to college), and at this point may be worthy of praise. But the doer can, and should, be encouraged from start to finish. Encouragement focuses on internal satisfaction opposed to external approval.

A TELLING (LITERALLY, TIME TELLING) EXERCISE

Praise is easy and quick to deliver. Hence, a significant reason for its popularity. It does not take a lot of effort, time nor brain matter to come up with a "Good Job," a "That's Tremendous," or a "Wow." On the other hand, encouragement makes you work a bit. It takes more time and effort to deliver.

Let's address the "time factor." My son completes his birdhouse and I praise his work, and by inference, him, by saying "Great job." That's it! It is a bit embarrassing to admit, but my response, "Great job," only took about a millisecond to think up and deliver. I, like most deliverers of praise, have had lots of practice at efficiently praising.

The "exercise," here, believe it or not, has already been partially completed. I saw the birdhouse in my son's hands, I know from experience that he would like a response from me, and in almost less time than it is possible to measure, I showered (really sprinkled) him with praise, "That looks great," on him. I would ask you to time how long it takes you to think up and deliver your praise, but you probably do not possess a watch that is that accurate. Let's just say that it was fast!

For the second part of the exercise, time how long it takes you to think up and deliver an encouragement statement. To complete this part of the exercise you will have to think of some specifics surrounding your son's efforts. You might recall that he was worried whether he could successfully follow the birdhouse plans. You might remember that he gave up going to the pool on Saturday in order to work on the project. You might recall that he labored over the size of the access hole for the birds of his choice, and for the best color paint or stain to use. Finally, you might recall that he entertained various options for how and where to suspend it in the back yard to thwart the always determined squirrels.

All these thoughts took you time to recall. They took further time to sort out which one or ones you would comment upon. In the meantime, you and your son are standing face to face, him with his birdhouse in hand. The pressure is on for your encouragement response. It is no wonder that it is so easy for some people to "cave in" and resort to sending praise.

The bottom line is that choosing and delivering an appropriate encouragement statement takes more time, energy, and creativity than that needed to deliver praise. You will have to decide whether it is worth it. But the payoff *is* worth it.

KEEPING OPEN THE LINES OF COMMUNICATION

In fact, the payoff for delivering encouragement is well worth it. Among other benefits to delivering encouragement, a primary one is that it has the potential to open and keep open communication between the person receiving the encouragement and the person delivering it. This does not happen with praise.

With praise, such as "That's great," "Wow," or "Great Job," once it is delivered there is very little else to say. The conversation, if there ever was one, is basically over. At most, the person receiving the praise may well utter, "Thanks." Your brief statement of praise, lacking any specifics that could be used for elaboration, suggests that you are not really tuned into his bird house building project.

Recalling some of the synonyms offered earlier for enthusiasm (i.e., bolster, galvanize), when it is delivered, an actual conversation is likely to follow. This conversation started now and perhaps, if time is tight, continued later, has the potential to empower your child – an attitude that will serve him in adulthood.

AURORA'S STORY – MOTHER TO DAUGHTER

This was another life-changing experience for your author. It centers around Aurora, the little daughter of a colleague, who was sitting in the dining room coloring, intense in her efforts for about a half hour. Aurora came out to the kitchen where her mother, Dawn, was working and excitedly proclaimed, "Look what I did. Look what I did!"

It is obvious that Aurora is expecting some sort of response from her mother. It is also clear that Aurora did not specifically ask for praise, she simply wanted her mother to share in her excitement about her colored drawing.

At this point Aurora's mother had a choice. She could deliver a statement of praise OR deliver a statement of encouragement. Let's look first at what might be common praise responses in this situation.

- "That's wonderful!"
- "That is absolutely tremendous!"
- "Wow! I've never seen anything that creative!"
- "It is one of the best pictures that I have ever seen!"
- "You are a great artist!"
- "I am very proud of you!"
- "You can really do super work if you put your mind to it!"
- "I am going to put right up on the refrigerator so that everyone can see it!"

No doubt her daughter would be tickled to hear such accolades. Aurora, even though young, probably knew that her mother has seen pictures that were more creative, ones that were better, knew that she was not really a "great artist," and that although, perhaps "tremendous," the drawing probably does not really qualify for "*absolutely* tremendous!"

The important point, though, is that all her mother's responses lacked an invitation to talk further about the drawing, or the effort, time and talent that went into creating it. What a wasted opportunity to engage one's child!

OK, you ask. What could Dawn have said to her daughter? Well, she could have delivered a plethora of encouraging responses. Please excuse my enthusiasm, but I don't get to use the word plethora very often – meaning abundance! Let's look at some of these encouragement responses.

- "Could you tell me about the picture?"
  [A simple but powerful and inviting response.]

- "I feel pretty special that you decided to share the picture with me. Thanks."
  [This simply acknowledges the fact that her child thinks his or parent is special.]

- "I see you put a lot of work into this. It looks like you really like to draw. Is that true?"
  [Notice the mother is not proclaiming that it IS true.]

- "You must feel pretty proud about doing this picture."
  [Note, you are asking, not telling the child that you are proud. A big difference!]

- "What was the hardest part about coloring the picture?"
  [All tasks have harder and easier parts. It helps to know the difference.]

- "How hard was it to stay within the lines? I don't think that I could have done that."

[Singles out a legitimate portion of the task that needed to be done right, but exactly how it can be done correctly demands some thought.]

- "How did you decide what colors to use?"
[No special answer is sought – but only the child knows the answer."]

- "What do you plan to do with the picture?"
[The parent may simply be curious."]

- "What other pictures are you thinking about drawing?"
[Again, the parent may simply be curious. But it gives her daughter an opportunity to think about and discuss future projects – if *she* wants to."]

- "Would it be OK with you if I put it up on the refrigerator?"
[As one "adult" to another, "Is it OK with you….." Seeking permission first.]

Note that these responses leave the conversation in the hands of Aurora. Her mother has offered a door-opener to talk further about her drawing. This offer treats Aurora as an equal, an experience many children do not have when surrounded by adults that only seem to judge and evaluate them.

Pay special attention to the last encouragement statement, the one dealing with placing the picture on the frig. Compare the encouragement approach to the praise approach. What is different? What is different is that with the encouragement statement, Aurora's mother asked permission to place the picture on the fridge door! Once again, Aurora is empowered to say OK or not OK.

VOTECH STORY – INSTRUCTOR TO TRAINEE

This story is similar in its intent to the Aurora Story. The reason for both stories, Aurora's and this one, is that these two stories are being used to help explain through examples what encouragement statements look like, how they differ from praise statements, and how they can be used to engage and empower the recipient.

A VoTtech student completes a meat tenderizer, a common project in machine shop. A block of aluminum, the future head of the tenderizer, must be machined on a lathe and cut to the size shown in the blueprints. Further, it must have milled knurled protrusions on both sides of the head (used to tenderize the meat), and have a hole drilled, with threads, to later accommodate the to-be-screwed-in handle. Next, the handle, itself, made of a piece of round stock aluminum, must be cut to length, and then threaded to exactly fit into the knurled head of the tenderizer. More knurls (to increase the grasp) must be milled into the handle. This project provides the student with a variety of machining skills.

At this point the student shows her completed meat tenderized to the instructor. Like Dawn, Aurora's mother in the previous example, the VoTech instructor has a choice on how to respond. He can deliver praise, or he can deliver encouragement. Let's look at examples of both. We will start with praise responses.

- "That's wonderful!"
- "I am very proud of you!"
- "You make me proud!"
- "It is one of the best projects I have seen in years!"
- "I knew that you were capable of doing such fine work!"
- "I am going to place it right over here in the display case for all to see!"

Like the Aurora story, there really is not much to say following the issued praise statements listed above. A student or trainee listening to these short, without a lot of thought statements, may infer that the instructor's intention is to close off communication as quickly as possible. Clearly, no invitation to talk, explain or question further has been offered.

Now, let's contrast these praise responses with encouragement responses. I will take a moment to comment on each encouragement response.

- "What was the most difficult part of the project?"

    [Anyone learning anything should be encouraged to analyze its difficulty for the next time. To be forewarned is to be forearmed.]

- "Can you suggest some ways in which I could better present the skills needed to complete this project?"

    [Who better to assist the instructor with his future planning than someone who just completed the project? The instructor's question conveys to the student a sense of equality – always conducive to promoting encouragement.]

- "How does it feel to work on a task for so long and finally complete it?"

    [The feeling of having completed a start-to-finish project, with one's "nose-to-the-grindstone," reinforces a sense of tenacity. It is a feeling that the student will repeatedly experience in the future.]

- "You must feel pretty good about your tool-and-die skills. Is that true?"

    [This gives the trainee an opportunity to discuss how he or she feels about the trade. Perhaps the instructor's question might help the student explore not only his or specific trade, but also explore how the tool-and-die skills might transfer to other trades.]

- "You probably will not be making this specific project for a career. What have you learned that can help you with future projects?"

[Encourages trainee to identify the specific skills required to complete not only the present project, but also future projects. Learning, in general, is not just about today, but more a preparation for tomorrow. What has been learned today will apply throughout one's career?]

- "What might change about how you would tackle such a project next time?"

    [All projects can be improved through reflection. Progress normally results from a series of both successes and failures – hence, the critical skill of self-examination.]

- "I appreciate your showing me your finished project. This helps reinforce my requiring this project as a good one for students. Thanks."

    [This shows the instructor's appreciation and reinforces the project's usefulness as a continued requirement for other students.]

- "Would it be O.K. with you if I put your project in the display case?"

    [Asking permission is just plain courteous. Further, it is what equals do! Of course, be prepared for the student to prefer the project not be displayed for all to see.]

- "May I send some lower-level students to you for help in completing their projects?"

    [Here the instructor is offering to share the role of "instructor." Learning theory tells us that we learn best by teaching others. This, then, is a win-win-win situation for the shop instructor (an extra pair of hands), the invited student co-instructor, and for other students who may need additional help. By the way, the student acting as co-instructor will look great on his or her future resume.]

ELEMENTARY SCHOOL STORY – TEACHER TO STUDENT

The previous two "stories," Aurora's and the Vo-Tech Trainee's, point out the contrast between the mother's and the instructor's responses – one of praising and one of encouraging. Here is a final example where we have a schoolteacher responding to a student. Given that this part of the book clearly is my effort to "sell" you on the value and virtues of encouragement, I will only highlight typical teacher encouragement, rather than praise, responses to a student.

Picture in your mind a classroom teacher sitting next to a little girl who has been working diligently on a writing assignment and who, now, is looking for supportive feedback from that teacher. This child could be your daughter, granddaughter, or niece.

Keep in mind that the teacher must work with a classroom full of students and, thus, cannot be at each student's side while he or she is working. Offering encouragement, as much and as often as possible, is a motivating tool that can aid, sustain and/or fortify a student to stick at the assigned task even when the instructor (or equivalent person) is not hovering at her side.

Note the several comments in brackets that follow a number of these encouragement responses. They were easy for your author to generate; they just seem to come naturally. Not so much, though, for statements of praise.

- "I noticed that you got right to work and got the whole assignment done. Good strategy!
  [Recognizes the value of effort and stick-to-it-ness.]

- "You used very descriptive words in your paragraph" It seemed to bring your story to life.

  [This is a recognition of eye-catching language.]

- "You've figured it out by yourself and stuck with it without giving up. That took focus!"

  [Like effort, sustained focus is crucial to any task. It should be learned early and experienced often.]

- "What did you learn from that mistake?"

  [Sometime mistakes are the best teacher.]

- "I've noticed how you've learned to use more adjectives. Do you think that it makes your writing more interesting to read?"

  ["Could you help me spice up a short piece that I am writing for my neighbor's small child? I think it could use more descriptive adjectives." Here the teacher is asking for the student to become the teacher and teach the teacher.]

- "I never thought about arranging the items that way. That looks eye-catching. How did you decide to do it that way?"

  [We can learn so much from others, even children.]

- "It looks as if you put a lot of work into that paper."

  [Nothing comes easy. Most tasks require hard work.]

- "You must be proud of the job you did on this."

  [Note, the student has the final say here.]

- "I see that you thought of a new way to connect the parts."

  [Helps student see value of thinking out-of-the-box.]

- "I appreciate the way that you worked with Angelo today. This helped her and it helped me – thank you."

[This is honest appreciation, not an attempt to manipulate. Usually, if you can end your delivered message with "Thank you," it is likely your message is one of encouragement and not praise.]

- "Suzie, tell me about your picture."
  [Who knows where this simple offer will lead? This is about as simple a message of encouragement as can be, but it is a very powerful encouragement message.]

TRY OUT ENCOURAGING FOR YOURSELF

Here is a letter your author received from one of his trainees. Perhaps the supplying of more encouragement and less praise will generate a similar "thank you" or two from an appreciative receiver of your bolstering, spurring, fortifying, and supporting encouragement messages.

> Dear Dr. Tauber,
>
> I wanted to say thanks for presenting the material on praise and encouragement. I never realized how much that I have used praise until your lecture. I made a conscious effort to use encouragement last night when talking to friends, and I can't believe the difference it made. They seemed more inspired and in control, plus it made me feel much better, too. Thank you again.

THE BOTTOM LINE

If you still feel compelled to deliver praise, at least avoid sending *inflated, gushy,* or *lavish* praise! An example of inflated praise would be, *"That was 'incredibly' good. It is beyond imagination!"* Instead, praise *effort*, not *ability, luck, intelligence,* or *cleverness.* An example of *effort* praise would be, "Wow! You really worked until you got it perfectly smooth. That took some real determination." Notice that there is no judgment or evaluation here, only a recognition of fact. Remember that *effort*, unlike *ability*, *luck*, *intelligence,* or *cleverness*, is the only attribution under the direct control of the person you are praising. *Effort* is like a home thermostat – it can be turned up or turned down. The other attributes are either static or simply out of reach.

MARIA MONTESSORI'S VIEW ON PRAISE

Maria Montessori, an educator, physician, and scientist in Italy started to investigate how best to help children learn – especially previously unschooled children. She had her work cut out for her. Today, Montessori schools, called Children's Houses, exist across the world, many here in the United States - available from preschool through high school. Her first US school opened in Scarborough, New York, in 1911. Your author's two children, David and Rebecca, both attended a Montessori School.

What is so unique about Montessori's approach to learning? First and foremost, there is no praise and no punishment! You heard me correctly. There are no external rewards, stickers or gold stars used to motivate learners. Instead, the work, itself, using apparatus (not called toys) such as the trinomial cube, the pink tower, the brown stairs, the cylinder blocks, the geometric tablets, and the triangular prism that the child chooses, focuses upon, and intensely works at until successful completion is, itself, internally rewarding! Further, what the children do as they interact with Montessori "didactic materials," meaning designed to teach, is their **work**. To label what they do as **play** would demean its importance. You would be insulted, and so would I, if people called our job or work simply playing.

The behaviorist-favored use of the carrot (i.e., praise) and the stick (i.e., punishment) approach is not used. It is not needed. At this point, you might be ready to scream, thinking how can children learn without praise (i.e., rewards) and punishment? Well, they can – and they do. Although not the primary focus of this book, do yourself a favor. Read a bit about Montessori education and then go visit a Montessori school. It will be a pleasant eye-opener.

All children have what Montessori calls an "absorbent mind." It is a special time in their lives where their mind is like a sponge – it so easily takes in the world around them – culture, language, music, math, science, etc. Your author has always been in awe of those who can master say Japanese, Chinese, Finnish or Hungarian. Yet, the youngest of children in those societies master their language with ease. I am still trying to master French and, yet I am lucky to be able to successfully order from a menu or ask the location of a toilet in Paris!

Montessori believes, and so does your author, that children, as well as adults, possess what psychologists call "epistemic curiosity," curiosity about knowledge. Children do not want to come inside to eat supper because investing the great outdoors is more stimulating. They don't want to stop and get their diapers changed because that would take away time from amassing knowledge. And, finally, they do not want to go to sleep at night because there is so much more to unravel about the world.

Children are internally driven to learn and can do much better when put in what Montessori calls a "prepared environment." Part of that "prepared environment" consists of being surrounded by Montessori apparatus, each designed to teach and/or reinforce a concept. Another part of that "prepared environment" consists of the messages that others (fellow students, his or her directress or director) deliver while he or she is learning. And, because learning is never finished (it is sort of like the infinite world of the internet), these delivered message are continually needed. Specifically, what messages are the best messages? The best messages given to any learner, child or adult are those that:

> bolster, buoy, fortify, inspire, impart resolution, help, soothe, cushion, sustain, assist, energize, champion, aid, support, fortify, shore up, restore, hearten, invigorate, enliven,

rekindle, stir, commiserate, spur, strengthen, rouse, inflame, boost, galvanize, awaken, embolden, revive, renew, cheer, console, and comfort.

If these messages look familiar, they should. You were introduced to them earlier as synonyms for that all-important message – encouragement!

SAMPLE WORDS OF ENCOURAGEMENT

As the next paragraph points out, there is always a danger that the message you intended to deliver is not the message actually received. To that end, one needs to be careful in the selection of his or her delivered words. Is what you are sending actually encouragement? Below are some examples of encouragement words that are less likely to be misinterpreted as praise words. You might note that all of these delivered words of encouragement have the potential of opening a dialogue – they send a message designed to invite further engagement, leaving it up to the receiver to decide what to say or do next.

"I'll bet you are proud of yourself!"
"You must have been practicing."
"Believe you can and you're halfway there."
"I feel honored that you shared your ideas with me."
"What was the most difficult part of the assignment."
"What are your plans for the next project?"
"Tell me about what you are doing."
"I'm curious, what do you think?"

WHEN ENCOURAGEMENT SOUNDING WORDS ARE REALLY PRAISE

A review of the literature reveals that some words offered by authors as examples of encouragement may actually be words of praise – with all of the negative baggage that carries. Delivered words such as "Sensational," "You are gifted," "I know that you will do great things." "You're amazing," ""What a super star you are," "I'm proud of the way you worked today," "I like how you think," and "You are a creative thinker," all are in danger of being perceived by the receiver as an evaluation, a manipulation, or as feedback about the person and not the all-important process that is responsible for any success. It is, of course, up to the receiver to determine whether a delivered message is praise or encouragement.

MORALIZING WORDS CONCEALED AS ENCOURAGEMENT

Too often when the going gets tough we are tempted to toss out the famous words, "The tough get going." Somehow these platitudes are supposed to help. Here are few more platitudes are supposed to carry the receiver over his or her occasional rough patches in life. What is there to say when these kinds of supposedly encouragement messages are delivered. Not much! One feels that one ought to pull himself up by his bootstraps, stop whining, and get on with life. If only life were all that simple. My favorite is, "Don't worry, be happy!" If life were only that simple.

Here are some others.

"Life is like a box of chocolates; you never know what you're going to get." (Sounds like Forrest Gump!)

"Good, better, best. Never let it rest. Till your good is better and your better is best." (St. Jerome)

"Nothing is impossible. The word itself says "I'm possible!"" Audrey Hepburn

"There is only one of you, so be yourself."

"You don't always need to follow the crowd."

"Your mistakes are chances to learn." [I should be a genius by now!]

"Challenges make you stronger."

"In time, you will feel better."

EXERCISE - RECOGNIZE PRAISE VERSUS ENCOURAGEMENT STATEMENTS

I suspect that by now you have grasped the clear difference between delivering praise and encouragement AND on the differences in impact that they offer. Let's now look at several scenarios where you are asked to recognize which of two presented responses is praise and which is encouragement.

Because the cost of inserting actual pictures (i.e., royalty rights, and typesetting) would have been prohibitive, I ask you to take a moment before responding and simply envision each of the following scenarios that follow.

After you have decided which statement is praise and which statement is encouragement, defend your selections. What, specifically, led you to identify one statement one way and another statement another way? Which response would best motivate the receiver?

Number 1

Jim, a 6th grade student, spent much of the afternoon helping the teacher clean up the art room. The area was especially messy because of the morning activities with the younger children. He picked up scraps, washed off the tables, and straightened the tables and chairs. His teacher responded:

a)_____ "The room was such a mess; it looks so clean and sparkling now. It's a pleasure to look at. Thanks!"

b)_____ "You are such a hard worker. I'm really pleased with the work that you did. You deserve something special."

Number 2

David was struggling with a math puzzle. After almost an hour of hard work, the pieces began to fall into place, and he found the solution. His grandma was watching from across the room and when he finished, she said:

a)_____ "David, you really struck to that puzzle until you had it solved. I was really happy for you when you found the solution."

b)_____ "David, I bet you are the only boy in the neighborhood who could solve that puzzle all by yourself. I'm really impressed."

Number 3

Sue lost her lunch money somewhere in the classroom. Her friend, Carol, happened to find it and gave it to her teacher. The teacher responded:

a)_____ "You are such an honest girl not to keep the money for yourself. I'm so proud of you!"

b)_____ "Sue will be so relieved that you found her money. You saved her a lot of trouble and worry."

Number 4

After much practice, Becky was able to play a complete song on the piano for the first time. She then played the song for her grandma. Her grandma responded:

a)_____ "I'm so proud of you. You must have a very special talent to be able to learn to play the piano so fast."

b)_____ "I really enjoyed listening to that song. Thanks for sharing it with me. I bet you are excited about the progress that you are making."

EXERCISE - YOUR TURN TO PRACTICE

The following are scenarios whereby someone is expecting a response from you. In real life, you have the choice to deliver either a praise *or* an encouragement response. Normally there is not time nor energy to deliver both. For this exercise, just for practice, let's supply *both* a praise *and* an encouragement response.

As in the previous exercise, take a moment to picture the circumstances surrounding each scenario prior to writing your response statement. In a real-life scenario, you probably would know a bit more about your grandchild's, friend's or neighbor's situation that should be a help in forming a quality response. Finally, take a moment, maybe one or two moments, to compose your response – especially your encouragement response – before delivering it. Write out your original responses.

- Ted and Alice (somewhere in their 50s) just completed a semester-long SCUBA diving class at the local community college. They showed their PADI card (wallet-sized diving certificate) to you. Your response is:

    Praise statement:

    Encouragement statement:

- Terry, your grandson calls you over at the beach to see his "almost completed" sand creation. What it is you don't really know, but he is excited about it. Your response is:

    Praise statement:

    Encouragement statement:

- Harold, a Montessori School student, has just completed the trinomial cube. He rang the bell, announcing that he would like some feedback. Note, at first glance it may appear that he simply completed a block-type puzzle. This apparatus exemplifies Montessori's way of introducing, in tangible form, algebra to the young child in the proof of the formula (a+b+c) to the third power! His teacher or classmate's response is:

  Praise statement:

  Encouragement statement:

- Your granddaughter has just figured out how the One Hundred Board works. She seems to be smiling ear to ear! As a loving grandparent your response is:

  Praise statement:

  Encouragement statement:

- Your grandson comes off the soccer field. His team has just lost the first game of the season. Your response is:

  Praise statement:

  Encouragement statement:

- Your brother, Randy, has just made it a full year without having a cigarette. As a caring sibling your response is:

  Praise statement:

  Encouragement statement:

- Your niece just phoned to tell you that she got accepted into her first-choice University. You understand that it was touch and go for a while. As a concerned grandparent your response is:

  Praise statement:

  Encouragement statement:

- Your neighbor calls you over to show you her first, ever, "Bird of Paradise" flower. Three years of trying to grow one seems to have finally paid off. As a good neighbor your response is:

  Praise statement:

  Encouragement statement:

- Your golf partner, Pam, has had, at least for her, a terrific drive that reached the green! More than once she had threatened to give up the sport. You respond by saying:

Praise statement:

Encouragement statement:

EXERCISE – PUT YOUR NEWFOUND KNOWLEDGE TO USE

Step outside into the real world. Look for opportunities to deliver response messages, both praise *and* encouragement. Start off sending, on purpose, a few praise statements and note the results – something you more than likely would not have done before being alerted to the cautions surrounding its delivery. Note how the people receiving your praise messages react. Do you, at best, get a return "thank you?" Does an awkward silence follow? Do you feel that once your praise has been delivered that there really is not that much more to say? Do you see, probably feel, one or more of the cautions happening?

Now, once again on purpose, send a few encouragement statements. As you form each message, ask yourself which of the synonyms for encourage do you want to stress – bolster, buoy, inspire, cushion, sustain, energize, invigorate, enliven, impart resolution, or offer comfort. Note how those receiving your encouragement messages react. Do you notice that your encouragement messages seem to encourage (no pun intended) the other person to say more? Do you notice any "temptation" on your part still to deliver long-honored praise messages?

Do you feel that you have helped the other person more with your encouragement messages than with your praise messages? Have you reached the point yet where you have decided to either stop, or at least significantly reduce, your use of praise as a response tool? Are you ready to commit to sending encouragement messages in the future?

CHAPTER 4

"He who praises everybody praises nobody."
(–Samuel Johnson)

Praising when the other person *does not* feel praiseworthy!

"LET ME KISS IT AND MAKE IT ALL BETTER!"

Yet, this is exactly the moment caring and concerned parents, spouses, teachers, and good friends whip out praise. For parents and children, we see the use of praise as sort of a "here, let be kiss it and make it all better."   This response may have worked for the occasional skinned knee when a child was young, but may no longer be the universal panacea or cure-all (like penicillin was once thought to be) for all unpraiseworthy feelings. Praising someone who does not feel praiseworthy, perhaps even also telling the person "You shouldn't feel that way," does little good.

The key word in the paragraph above is that the other person does not FEEL praiseworthy. These strong FEELINGS can be debilitating. They can stand in our way of getting on with the trials and tribulations of daily life. Life does not simply stand still while we try to get our act together. Feelings, especially intense feelings, must be handled, not simply "kissed away with praise." But feelings can be "listened" away or at least "listened" away to the point that they are more under a person's control.

Confucius once said (actually it is your author who has repeatedly said), "The problem with the problem is not the problem. The problem with the problem is the strong feelings surrounding the problem. That's the problem!" Two people can have the same minor fender bender. The first person, experiencing sleepless nights, lets it shape her life, vowing never to drive again. The second person says to herself, s--- happens. I'm physically fine, and although an inconvenience to repair, I have insurance." Same exact problem; two very different sets of feelings!

Unless the underlying feelings are addressed and helped to come to the surface so that they *can* be addressed, their power to debilitate will continue. Praise does little, if anything, to bring these underlying feelings to light. Listening, on the other hand, does. It empowers the person who owns the problem. Ownership of a problem is a prerequisite to handling a problem and the accompanying debilitative feelings.

What specific feeling are we talking about when we note that someone does not feel praiseworthy? Like layers of an onion, the real feeling may reside below several layers that need to be peeled off. Too often, even the person who owns the problem is unable to diagnose it at first glance. Surely, we would not be so arrogant as to think that our praising could address all debilitating feelings.

SYNONYMS FOR FEELING UNPRAISEWORTHY

Here are just some of the feelings that can manifest themselves in the generic feeling of not feeling praiseworthy. Which feeling is the right feeling? Only the person who owns the problem can answer this question. Once answered one is well on his or her way to dealing more effectively with that feeling(s).

Overwhelmed, Sad, Envious, Left-Out, Angry, Depressed, Miserable, Disappointed, Forlorn, Mournful, Dejected, Miserable, Unhappy, Glum, Pensive, *Why Me*? Terrible, Distressed, Lonely, Mischievous, Cheerless, Forlorn, Heartbroken, Dejected, Fed Up, Down in the Dumps, Low, Pessimistic, Downhearted, Inferior, Stupid, Inept, Unloved, Apathetic, and many more!

SON AND DAD DIALOGUE

The scene. A young son, say 8 years old, comes into the room crying. His dad tries to help his son with, at this point, an unknown problem. All we know is that something is bothering the child enough to cause him to be in tears.

Dad: "Hey, what's up?"
Son: "Nothing…"
Dad: "Come on now, what's bothering you?"
Son: "The coach didn't pick me for the soccer team!"
Dad: "But you are one of the best players on the team. I've watched your practices, and you are a great soccer player. Boy, the coach will be sorry he didn't pick you!"
Son: (thinking) "I know dad is just trying to make me feel better, but the coach says I am not good enough and dad says I am great. Someone is lying to me. Who should I believe?"

This little dialogue dance continues, as it does in most homes. The dad tries to use praise to wipe away his son's tears and unworthiness feeling. That is his role in this dance. The child, too, has a role. His role is to pretend that his dad's praise has made him feel better. This, of course, will act as a reward for the dad who, then, will be more likely to use praise in the future to try and wipe away his son's pain.

The problem is that nothing has been solved in the son's life. The problem is still there – he still did not get on the soccer team. Further, the son now faces the dilemma of whom to believe, his coach or his dad. One of them is lying. And, finally, probably most serious of all in the son's mind is that he is no better prepared, come Monday morning when he returns to school, to "face the music," to face the fact that everyone in the school knows that he did not get selected for the team. What's he going to do to save face? Perhaps he could walk down the hall and loudly proclaim, "At least my dad thinks I am a great soccer player." I am, of course, only kidding with this last utterance. Nowhere on God's green earth would a student make such a proclamation.

SO! HOW SHOULD YOU RESPOND?

Let's take a real situation, one where your young child comes running into the kitchen, crying, and blurts out, "Johnny won't play with me. He is just an old stinkbug! I hate him!" At this point there is enough evidence to conclude that he feels unpraiseworthy – his best friend does not want to play with him. Clearly, praise is not going to solve the problem.

This scenario, and millions like it, occur day after day. How should we respond? Unfortunately, too many parents (and others in other scenarios) respond by sending roadblocks to communication, work introduced by Thomas Gordon in his *PET: Parent Effectiveness Training* and *TET: Teacher Effectiveness Training* books and workshops offered across the globe.

Here is what Gordon found to be *ineffective* in helping people handle their strong-feelings problem. All 12 of these responses are roadblocks to communication. You will notice that delivering praise is one of them - #7.

ROADBLOCKS TO COMMUNICATION

I will leave it to the reader to research, via a simple Google search, concrete examples of these 12 roadblocks to communication. Once again, this list presents what NOT to do when someone does not feel praiseworthy. (Yep, I know. There are two negatives in the preceding sentence.) The solutions that follow this list of what not to do address what one should do. Basically, it tells you to listen!

1. Ordering, Directing
2. Warning, Threatening
3. Moralizing, Preaching
4. Advising, Giving Solutions
5. Persuading with Logic, Arguing
6. Judging, Blaming
7. **Praising, Agreeing**
8. Name-calling, Ridiculing
9. Analyzing, Diagnosing
10. Reassuring, Sympathizing
11. Probing, Questioning
12. Being Sarcastic, Humor, Diverting

There is not enough time to address these "what not to do's" in depth. Suffice it to say, you are more of a help when you listen – actively listen – than when you talk! Active listening empowers a person, it keeps the person with the problem in control. And, as he or she can solve (or at least handle) the debilitating feelings surrounding today's problem, the experience helps him or her to get ready for tomorrow's problems.

ALTERNATIVES TO ROADBLOCKS TO COMMUNICATION

- Silence
  Be there for the person who does not feel praiseworthy.
  Look interested, be interested, be quiet, lean slightly forward,

uncross your closed posture arms and legs, do not repeatedly check your watch so as to convey a signal to the problem owner to stop talking.

- Door-Openers
  How does the person with the problem know whether you have the time or the interest in hearing him or her out? One of the simplest ways to know is to ask, *"Would you like to talk about it?"* Even if the person does not take you up on your offer this time, you have sent a clear message. You have just told the person that if he or she does want to talk in the future, you would be willing to listen. He or she will save your invitation!

- Non-Committal Responses – basically *"grunting*!" or saying, *"no kidding"* and *"wows."*
  Do not sell these responses short. They can be very powerful, especially if delivered at the right time with the right emphasis. Further, they tell the listener that, unlike staying silent, you are "with him or her." Otherwise, how would you have known the precise moment to *"grunt"* or say *"my, my, that actually happened*?"

- Active Listening: Listen for the person's feelings and then reflect them!
  Explained further immediately below.

ACTIVE LISTENING - AN EMPATHETIC SKILL

We have two ears but only one mouth! There is probably a reason for this. We should talk less and listen more. Yet, most people do not know how to active listening. They have not been trained to do it, it has not been modeled for them by parents, teachers, coaches, and bosses, and to some it defies their natural urge to step in and "do something" to solve the problem even though it not their problem!

Active listening takes the form of non-committal responses. The person with the problem (i.e., not feeling praiseworthy) talks and the listener reflects. The listener does not add his or her "two-cents" worth. This can be liberating to problem owners who have been surrounded by good intentioned problem solvers all their lives.

Reflective counseling, or active listening, acts as a sound board (i.e., the surface of a guitar that the strings vibrate against) helping to amplify the problem holder's feelings so that he or she (not necessarily you) can better "hear" them. As with a guitar, plucking the stings in mid air makes little or no sound. But, when attached to a sound board and plucked, they can easily be heard.

Non-committal responses leave the ball in the court of the person who owns the problem. The person with the problem can take it in any direction he wants, stay there if he wishes, and conclude the session whenever desired.

Here are sample active listening, reflective, and non-committal responses that one might deliver to someone who owns a problem – including the problem of not feeling praiseworthy.

- "It sounds like you are really feeling…."
  > [There is no claim made here that the listener knows for sure what the actual feeling is. The problem owner can respond, if he so chooses, with *"Yeh, Yeh, that's it"* or *"No. It is more like such and such…"* It is her choice.]

- "What I hear you saying is…. Is that right…."
  > [Once again, the listener offers at best a tentative response making it clear that the problem owner, and only the problem owner, knows for sure."

- "Wow. That actually happened….?"
  > [This is a response that tries to reflect the intensity of the owner's conveyed problem.]

- "I see...." "Really...." "Oh..." "No fooling...."
    [These are non-committal "grunts" that keep the
    conversation going IF that is what the person with the
    problems wants.]

- "Gee, you don't seem yourself today...."
    [Often people with problems are hoping that someone
    will notice their atypical behavior and make this
    observation. Most problem owners are not "brave
    enough" to come right out and say, "I have such and
    such problem, will you listen to me?"]

- "It looks like something is really bothering you...."
    [A message that you have noted what could be a
    problem and you stand ready to listen.]

- "I'm not sure, but it sounds like you...."
    [All active listening responses are tentative, at best.]

- "Want to talk about it.... I'm all ears...."
    [Clearly a door-opener being offered.]

- "Your words say one thing, but your body says...."
    [Often one's body can send a plea for help when
    one's words, at first, may seem too scary or
    humiliating to utter.]

Active listening keeps the person who owns the problem
talking, all the while knowing that the listener is not sitting in
judgment. It feels safe because it is safe. We all either know from
personal experience with therapists, or from having watched our fair
share of movies where one or more characters are in therapy, that
what the best therapists do best is to listen – not talk! If one *must*
talk, that talk should be encouraging, not praising.

Empathetic listening, the number one skill of great leaders, is
encouraging in large part because it sets the stage for engagement

between a deliverer and receiver. Although not all problems can be solved by delivering encouragement, the fact is that encouragement paves the way for a dialogue without any manipulation, control, moralizing, or any of the other roadblocks to communication presented earlier.

Two resources of your author that the reader may find useful are:

- *Delivering Empathy: Fundamental to Successful Leadership!*

- *Using Empathy as Physicians: The What, Why, and How!*

CHAPTER 5

"I love criticism just so long as it is unqualified praise."
(– Noel Coward)

Praising when the other person *does* feel praiseworthy!

FEELING GREAT CAN BE DEBILITATING!

Sometimes people feel so great about something that they cannot get on with life's responsibilities until they get themselves "talked down." Talking to a wall is not very helpful; we normally prefer talking to a person! Believe it or not, feeling praiseworthy can be just as debilitating as feeling unpraiseworthy – both situations demand that those feelings be handled. It shouldn't need to be said, but praising someone who already feels praiseworthy, is a bit redundant – he or she already feels praiseworthy. How much more praiseworthy can one feel than to feel praiseworthy? It would be a bit overkill – like the cold war between the Soviet Union and the USA. We each possessed a stockpile of nuclear weapons that could have destroyed each other's cities many times over. How many times can one take out another country's capital?

Years ago, I had a short manuscript accepted for publication in *Phi Delta Kappan*, a respected journal in my discipline. This was, at least in my mind, a real accomplishment. I just had to share the great news. I could have shared the news with colleagues, but in the world of publish or perish, had I bragged about the acceptance this would have meant that my publication record was now stronger in comparison to my peers. Believe me, colleagues do not want to hear this. So, what did I do? It was late in the afternoon, so I drove home, and unable to share the news with my wife who was still at her teaching job, I sat our dog, Ginger, down and shared the news with her – really! Not a jealous bone in her body, just a wagging tail and a lick or two to my face. It felt wonderful. Realty then set in, and I returned to the daily demands of life. I took out the garbage.

PEOPLE SEEKING THEIR "15 MINUTES OF FAME"

Let me present one thing that you should not do when responding to someone who already feels praiseworthy. What follows is a major "don't!"

Don't stand there just waiting for the other person to take a breath and then use that opportunity to chime in with what you believe is your "even more exciting moment" in life! "Gee, you think your operation was painful, let me tell you all about mine!" Or, "You think your recent cruise to the Caribbean was great, let me tell you about mine!" This is called "one-ups-man-ship." It tries to steal the show, it tries to pull the rug out from under the person who feels praiseworthy and wants, at least for a moment or two, to have his or her "15 minutes of fame," and it is just plain rude.

What does someone look like when they are seeking their "15 minutes of fame?" The signs are obvious whether you examine your own behavior and demeanor or that of another person. Symptoms consist of, among others, "levitating" an inch or two above the floor, appearing almost breathless, rapid speech, exaggerated motions, and sparkling eyes. It would not be unusual for you, or another the person seeking his or her "15 minutes of fame," to come right out and say, "I just have to tell someone!"

The following several stories describe where one person feels particularly praiseworthy and simply wants his or her moment in the limelight – his or her 15 minutes of fame. Offering encouragement responses, from the simplest, "Tell me all about it," are a tried-and-true way to help the person revel in the limelight.

Gene Hackman in *Hoosiers*

There are not a lot of inspirational movies that I watch over and over, but one of them is the 1986 sports film, *Hoosiers*, starring Gene Hackman. It is based loosely on a small rural school basketball team that ended up, as underdogs, winning the 1954 Indiana State Championships

In the movie there is an emotional scene outside the classrooms of teacher, Norman Dale (Gene Hackman) and teacher, Myra Fleener (Barbara Hershey), where Hackman confronts her because she had persuaded the star basketball player, Jimmy Chitwood, to quit basketball and focus on his studies. Hackman tries to explain that this moment in time may be that one and only moment in the players' lives that is their "15 minutes of fame." The message, here, is that when someone feels praiseworthy, let them, in fact, help them, experience their "15 minutes of fame." Don't steal their thunder. This would equate to one-ups-man-ship. Maybe, next time they can help you with your "15 minutes of fame" – but not right now at this moment! This is their time.

Al Bundy in *Married with Children*

I almost am reluctant to offer this second example of where someone tries to cling to his one and only "15 minutes of fame." This is the story of the television program, *Married with Children*, where the shoe salesman, father, Al Bundy's "15 minutes of fame" is that while attending Polk High School he scored four touchdowns in a single game! This may be his highlight in his life. Don't spoil it for him. Let him, help him, relive this special time in his life if he wishes to do so. Your turn can follow.

Dr. Kallgren's "Hovering on Air"

Dr. Kallgren, a colleague of mine, came bounding into my office one day excitedly waving a copy of a prestigious Psychology journal in my face. He seemed to be hovering, without one of today's actual hoverboards, just a few inches above the floor. How he could hover, I did not know. I asked the same question that you probably would have asked. "What's up?" At that point Dr. Kallgren went on to show me (he had highlighted it!) that in three places within the article a rather famous Psychology author had cited his research. He just had to tell someone. I guess that I was handy and, of course, would understand his excitement.

At that moment Dr. Kallgren's feet gently settled back down to the floor and off he went to tackle, in comparison, the mundane responsibilities of the rest of the day. Think of how deflating it would have been to him if I had taken that very opportunity to practice "one-ups-man-ship" and showed him my recently published textbook. He wanted, and I helped provide, his "15 minutes of fame." It took less than five minutes. By the way, I did verbally respond to his excitement, not by praise, but by supplying encouragement. I said, "Hey, isn't the work he is citing part of that research that you struggled over all last year and on more than one occasion were ready to throw in the towel?" I reinforced his being in control of his own destiny, and I acknowledged his stick-to-it-ness. I did not praise him.

My Personal Example – Still Hurts Even Today

I have a personal example to offer of feeling praiseworthy and looking for someone to help me experience my "15 minutes of fame." At one point during my career as a professor I had two books published that came out the same week. Believe me this has *never* happened again. I had the two books with me when I joined a colleague at a neighborhood watering hole. Here we were sitting at the bar talking and watching a hockey game (of no real importance to either of us), when I showed him the two books. I was primed and ready to get my "15 minutes of fame."

To quote the author, again, "The problem with the problem is not the problem. The problem with the problem is the strong feelings surrounding the problem. That's the problem!" I was experiencing very strong, although not clearly identified, feelings. How was I feeling just before my praiseworthy feelings were ignored? Here are just some of the feelings that can manifest themselves in the generic feeling of feeling praiseworthy. I had most of them!

Happy, Ecstatic, Joyous, Delighted, Satisfied, Jubilant, Elated, Pleased, Thrilled, Chipper Tickled Pink, Overjoyed, Euphoric, Pleased, Radiant, Excited, Over the Moon, On Cloud Nine, Effervescent, Happy as a Clam, and many more.

What happened? Nothing happened. Basically, all he did was to say "Great" (with little enthusiasm) and then turned his attention back to the tv. It would have been nice to have someone (i.e., my colleague in this case) help me explore these positive feelings for a moment or two. As you can tell, I felt shortchanged and, twenty years later, I still feel shortchanged. I know you are thinking, "Get over it!"

Patting yourself on the back when you definitely feel praiseworthy is not only very difficult to physically do, but also just not the same as when another person does it to you or with you. I suppose, feeling really praiseworthy is a bit like having sex – it is normally better with two people!

Your **Personal Example?**

What is an example of where you think that you were denied your "15 minutes of fame?" I'm sure that you have one (or more) example. What had you achieved or what had you accomplished that you just had to share with someone? But, when you tried, that someone did not appear all that interested in your achievement even though you had sent obvious cues that you wanted to "brag" for a moment or two. Perhaps, even worse, did the person you turned to attempt to steal the show by playing one-ups-man-ship with his or her story?

CONCLUSION

Perhaps the word "conclusion" misrepresents your author's intended message. A better word might be "beginning." For those of you who already supply encouragement to others, I say "Keep it up, champion its use, be a role model for it, spread the word!" For those of you who, after reading this book, have been persuaded to switch sides, from praise to encouragement, I say "Welcome to the fold. You and those you encourage, will be better for it." For those of you still hooked on supplying praise, I say check your motives for doing so and, if you must supply it, avoid delivering inflated praise.

The bottom line. Just because you think you are delivering encouragement, just because you say you are delivering encouragement, does not make it so! It is only encouragement *if* it meets the accepted definition, offered earlier in this book, for encouragement. Otherwise, at best (maybe at worst) you are actually delivering praise, a response most known for its ability to evaluate or judge another person.

When you listen to those who have made a conscious, informed decision to use encouragement, you often hear them admit, "I am committed to supplying encouragement, but every so often I catch myself sliding back to using praise." But, **not once**, **not ever**, have I heard someone say, "I now am committed to supplying praise, but every so often I catch myself sliding back to the use of encouragement." The words "sliding back" never are used when referring to the word encouragement.

TAKE THE 85% - 90% CHALLENGE!

A common outcome that occurs when people have digested the differences between praise and encouragement is that they often "change sides." Every time your author has conducted a workshop, class, or seminar on this topic, when asked at the end of the session, "How many of you plan to either stop using, or at least significantly reduce using, praise," 85% to 90% of the audience raises their hands. This 85% to 90% outcome has *never* failed to emerge.

I realize that because you may be reading this book alone that it is impossible for you to check out for yourself this outcome. You may just have to take my word for it. Just out of curiosity, are you among those who have a "change of heart" regarding the use of praise?

ASSIGNMENT FOR NEXT TIME (with another person)

What would be ideal would be to teach the material in this book via two sessions. The first session would point out how praise and encouragement differ, point out the cautions regarding the use of praise, and then offer encouragement as a problem-free alternative. This is, in effect, what I have tried to do in this book.

At the end of the first session an assignment would be made. The assignment would involve going out into the real world and "testing" both the cautions regarding the use of praise and the impact of offering its substitute – encouragement. You would be asked to record the results of your praise and encouragement responses for analysis in a follow-up second session.

Specifically, such an assignment would direct you to:

- Note situations where you were the recipient of praise or encouragement messages.

- Note how you reacted to these delivered praise and encouragement messages
- Look for opportunities to deliver praise and encouragement messages.
- Note how those receiving your praise or encouragement messages react.
- Note how well your delivered messages keep the lines of communication open.
- Note any "temptation" on your part to revert to long-honored praise messages.
- Summarize your overall reaction to the use of praise and encouragement.
- Be prepared to share your efforts and observations in next week's class.
- Finally, if you are among the 85% - 90% of the readers who have had a change of heart regarding the supplying of praise, spread the word to others.

Have fun! Have more fun!
Remember, "Fun is nature's reward for learning!"

Now that you have finished reading this book, except for the annotated bibliographic entries that follow, and hopefully taken the 85% - 90% challenge, would you be kind enough to share your thoughts with me?

- Have your views on delivering praise been altered?
- Were the 21 Cautions presented in this book convincing?
- Are you ready to embrace encouragement as a preferred alternative to praise?
- Please send me a brief email indicating your current beliefs regarding praise and encouragement. I can be reached at rtt1453@comcast.net.
- Thank you.

CHAPTER 6

"Too much praise makes you feel you must be doing something
terribly wrong!"
(–Dorothy Day)

OTHERS WHO RECOGNIZE THE CAUTIONS BEHIND DELIVERING PRAISE

Let the Research Speak!

Your author is not alone in believing that one should be cautious when delivering praise – especially to children. What follows is just a smattering of respected journal articles where the problems associated with praise are addressed. It is, on one hand, staggering that so much has been written about the possible damage of supplying praise and, on the other hand, how popular the use of praise remains.

Review these resources. Get on your tablet or computer, secure copies of them, read them and digest them. You will find many of the same messages (e.g., cautions) regarding the use of praise. Despite the overwhelming challenges to the use of praise, do not be discouraged. Why? You have a perfectly good alternative behavior at your disposal – ENCOURAGEMENT.

Will the world stop spinning if you continue to deliver praise? Probably not! But now that we know the power of encouragement and the fact that it is impossible to negatively impact someone by delivering it, it begs the question. Why not substitute encouragement for praise?

Further, the laws of physics say that two objects (or actions) cannot occupy the same space at the same time. Hence, every time that you expend time and energy delivering praise is an opportunity that you could have used to deliver encouragement.

Finally, please note that these resources are alphabetically listed and represent relatively current citations. Having said that, I want to point out what appears to be a dated, yet often cited, 1963 article by Richard E. Farson, titled "Praise Reappraised." It appeared in volume 4, number 5, of the *Harvard Business Review*. No review of praise would be complete without a reference to this article. The original article is well worth your read. The author starts off his article "beginning to question the cherished idea that people enjoy being praised."

- 1) Alfano, Andrea. (2015). Too Much Praise Promotes Narcissism. *Scientific American.* June 1.
  [A longitudinal study of children supports the theory that parents with unrealistically positive views of their children foster narcissistic qualities. At first, it may seem cute when children act self-centered, but what are parents are doing their children by praising such behavior.]

- 2) Amster, Sara-Ellen. (1994). The Case Against Praise and Rewards: A Conversation with Alfie Kohn. *Harvard Education Letter*. 10(2).

    [Referencing Alfie Kohn's work, the author states that rewards (no matter their form) and punishments are not opposites - just two sides of the same coin. The author notes that at least we have half the battle won – more enlightened people are likely to acknowledge the downside to punishment.]

- 3) Bailey, Richard. (2014). The Problem with Praise. *Psychology Today*. November 1.

    [Research appears to challenge the recommended pedagogical practice of praising students lavishly – a technique seen as a core strategy of teachers, parents, and coaches. Statistics reveal that youngsters are becoming put off from participating in sports due, in part, to the over-emphasis on winning.]

- 4) Baumeister, Roy., Hutton, Debra., and Cairns, Kenneth. (1990). Negative Effects of Praise on Skilled Performance. *Basic and Applied Social Psychology*. 11(2):131-148.

    [The authors conducted a series of experiments to investigate the possibility that praise could, in some circumstances, impair subsequent performance. One conclusion was that praise seems to increase effort, but it may also hinder skilled performance.]

- 5) Belluck, Pam. (2000). New Advice for Parents: Saying 'That's Great!' May Not Be. *The New York Times*, October 18.

    [The article reports on the value of consciously avoiding sending praise and, instead, responding with messages designed to encourage learners. She argues that lavish and frequent praise can turn students into praise junkies.]

- 6) Bailey, Richard (2014). The Problem with Praise: Praise Is Not Always a Good Thing. November 1.

    [Praise that is intended to be encouraging for low-attaining students may convey a message of low expectations. When students are praised for their successful performance on an easy task, it could be evidence of the teacher's lower expectations for them – hence, their self-esteem can drop.]

- 7) Bertelsmann, Margot. (2016). Are You Over-Praising Your Child? *Parent24*. September 13.

  [Today's parents, operating on a backlash from the harsh, authoritarian, parenting styles of the past, tend to overindulge in delivering praise. Experiments reveal that children, especially those with a lower self-esteem, who receive inflated praise are less willing to tackle more difficult tasks in the future for fear of making mistakes.]

- 8) Biaso, M. (2007). Does Praise Set Kids Up to Fail? *Free Republic*. August 15.

  [Constant praise can give someone an unhealthy sense of entitlement. Generic praise, the most often form of it delivered, fails to encourage (the focus of this book) hard work, effort, and determination. After all, if one is "entitled" to praise then why should one have to work hard for it?]

- 9) Black, Susan. (2000). The Praise Problem. *School Board Journal*. 187(8):38-40.

  [Praise is widespread and deeply woven into daily classroom practice. But when praise is overused, it can do harm. If one is going to praise, it should be directed towards a student's efforts, not his intelligence or cleverness.]

- 10) Bright Horizons (2012). The Benefits of Encouragement vs. Praise. *Brighthouse horizons*.

  [Dweck's widely cited research on praise is stressed. Related to the focus of our book, the author recommends that as an alternative to praise we should offer encouragement. Further, also noting the emphasis of our book, although encouragement may take more time and effort to deliver, it is worth the effort.]

- 11) Bronson, Po. (2007). How Not to Talk to Your Kids: The Inverse Power of Praise. *New York Magazine*. August 3.

  [Dweck's research is cited. The case of Thomas, a child who has been told from birth that he is intelligent, is explored. Observations of Thomas revealed that his persistence at a task was lowered when the task was not easily and quickly mastered.]

- 12) Chambers, Y. S. (????). Stop praising kids and start doing this instead. KiddieMatters (kidiematters.com).

  [Chambers' article pretty much mirrors many of the cautions cited in Tauber's book. Our reliance on delivering praise appears to be an outgrowth of the 80's and 90's self-esteem movement. The Chambers' alternative to delivering praise is to deliver encouragement. Many concrete examples of delivering encouragement instead of praise are cited.]

- 13) Chambers, Y. S. (????). The difference between praise and encouragement. KiddieMatters (kidiematters.com).

   [Chambers argues that praise comes with a judgment ("I like how you...," "I'm so proud of you.") and, thus, denies the other person the opportunity to figure out what is important to him or her. She points out that, of course, we should limit our delivery of praise, but we also should be careful not to over-encourage. Chambers offers a list of 25 encouragement statements that one could deliver. She points out that children, especially, undervalue effort and hard work, mistakenly believing that success or failure is based solely on intelligence and natural talent.]

- 14) Childcare (2019). Encouragement is More Effective in Guiding Children's Behavior. *childcare.extension.org*. August 15.

   [Many childcare providers try to help children feel more confident by praising them. Yet, supplying encouragement actually is more effective than praise in doing so. And, when a little bit of praise does not work, the adult is likely to increase its frequency and intensity. But overpraising can lower a child's self-esteem and make them, among other factors, more competitive and less cooperative.]

- 15) Dix, Paul. (2015). I Hate Your Praise! – What You Do When a Child Doesn't Want to Hear Compliments? *Teachwire.* November 3.

   [Most children swell with pride when you acknowledge their 'over and above' performance, so says Dix. But there are some children who don't like receiving it at all. What are you to do? The author explains what to do and what not to do.]

- 16) Dweck, Carol S. (1999). Caution – Praise Can Be Dangerous. *American Educator.* 23(1):1-5.

   [Like others, this author traces our feeling that we should lavish praise on children to the self-esteem movement. The goal of helping children raise their self-esteem is important to Dweck, it is just the method of trying to raise it, relying on praise, that she questions. She notes that praise is actually the "chief weapon" in the hands of those trying to raise self-esteem."]

- 17) Dweck, Carol S. (2007). The Perils and Promises of Praise. *Educational Leadership*. 65(2):34-39.
  [No one has written more about, and got us re-examining, the supplying of praise to children. We seemed to have reached a point where children expect praise because they are special, not because of the effort they have put forth. A discussion of whether praise is fixed or malleable, followed by the two faces of effort, are presented. As always, her articles are well referenced.]

- 18) Dweck, Carol S. (2008). Mindsets: How Praise is Harming Youth and What Can Be Done About It? *School Library Media Activities Monthly*. 24(5):55-58.
  [Student, and later, worker, self-esteem may or may not actually be strengthened, but one thing for sure is that young people seem to need constant praise. If praise is to be offered, it should be effort-praise. This form of praise helps maintain the receiver's faith in his or her own ability and enjoyment doing the task. The outcome, over time, is marked improvement in performance.]

- 19) Elicay, Kitty (2019). How to praise your child makes a huge difference in his life: 6 ways to do it right. *Smart parenting*. March 23.
  [As the author of this book, I was reluctant to include this brief article as it seems to suggest that if only one delivers praise the "right way" then any praise cautions would disappear. The author cites, "Be honest" – always a great idea, "Encourage effort, not talent" – effort is the only factor under a child's control, "Be specific" – "you're awesome" denies the child an opportunity to analyze what went so well, "Stop comparing" – "give it your all" is all that a child can do, "Don't use encouragement (or praise) to control" – yet this often is the number one goal of its delivery, and "Avoid Overpraising" – "why try harder when I apparently am already doing a fantastic job?"]

- 20) Elkins, Robert. (1981). Too Much Praise is Abuse. *Educational Leadership*. 38(6):482.
  [The reliance upon teachers delivering praise starts early in their teacher training. But, argues the author, what are the consequences to their effusive praise? Instead of teaching students

that true evaluations come from inside an individual, the reliance upon praise sends the opposite message – evaluation must come from some authority figure.]

- 21) Encouragement vs. Praise. (2016). Twin Parks Montessori Schools. November 16.

  [The author reflects upon her early parenting where the so-called experts of the time said to accentuate the positive and go heavy on the praise. That she did. After learning about the Montessori approach, the contrast between extrinsic and intrinsic motivation became clear. She now favors the latter.]

- 22) Encouragement vs. Praise: What's the Difference? *acecqa.gov.au*.

  [It is through receiving encouragement, not praise, that individuals gain a more accurate picture of what their own, not someone else's, competencies and qualities are. Citing Alfie Kohn, the author points out that praise: manipulates children, creates praise junkies, steals a child's pleasure, reduces a child's interest, and reduces a child's achievement.]

- 23) Encouragement vs. Praise: Why the Differentiation Matters. (XXXX). *Positive Parenting Solutions*.

  [The author makes a number of points challenging the value of praise. Among them are praise is superficial, focuses on the doer, not the deed ("You are awesome!), and decreases internal motivation and confidence. This is followed by how to more effectively deliver encouragement. One particular response to be avoided is to "piggyback" in the form of following your message with an "I told you so!" Your encouragement then feels like a "jab in the gut!]

- 24) Fernandes, D. (2013). Researchers Say Too Much Praise Harms Kids; Parents Hear: blah, blah, blah. *Scpr.org*. August 14.

  [When picking up their toddlers, parents were handed a surprising note – it said stop constantly praising your child! The question of using praise to boost a child's self-esteem is questioned. Encouraging children, the focus of our book, is offered to keep a child engaged and to understand that learning can be hard work – it can take grit.]

- 25) Flanagan, Alex. (2018). Stop Praising Kids with "Good Job"! *Balance*. May 4.

  [The author contrasts two situations – one where a child hits a home run and another when a child strikes out. Yet, both receive screams of "Good Job" from the bleachers. Someone is lying. Kids know this, they are not dumb. Saying "good Job" when by any measure it is not true relegates future "Good Jobs" from you as just background noise.]

- 26) Fogg, Ally. (2014). The Art of Praising Children – and Knowing When Not to. *The Guardian*. January 7.

  [The author describes his own reaction to a "painting" his young son shares with him. In truth, it is not all that good. Do I lavish praise on him? Further reading by this author revealed that the research is clear, unearned extravagant praise on a kid may do more harm than good. It appears praise is not a universal motivator.]

- 27) Lepper, Mark., and Green David. (1974). Turning Play into Work Effects of Adult Surveillance and Extrinsic Rewards on Children's Intrinsic Motivation. *Journal of Personality and Social Psychology*. 31(3):479-486.

  [As it relates to praise, a form of reward, the authors found that preschool children who had undertaken an earlier activity expecting an extrinsic reward showed less subsequent interest in that activity than did those who had not expected a reward.]

- 28) Grey, Kathleen. (1995). Not in Praise of Praise. Part of a training kit from ChildCare Information Exchange.

  [Describes a "kit" that can be used to better understand the advantages and disadvantages of delivering praise. Practice changing praise statements into encouraging (reflection) statements is addressed.]

- 29) Grille, Robin. (2007). Rewards and Praise: The Poisoned Carrot. *The Natural Child Project*.

  [On one had the author claims that praise-and-reward is backed up by a ton of research and hints that that should instill confidence in its use. On the other hand, the bulk of the research springs from the work of psychologists showing that through painstaking work, lab rats, pigeons, and dogs can be trained. In real life such conditioning with children creates jealousy, envy, and mistrust.]

- 30) Gfroerer, Kelly. (2020). What is the Difference Between Praise and Encouragement? *CONTINUED*. December 11.

    [We live in a praise-focused culture – so says the author. The contrast between praise and encouragement is helped by shifting from, "I like," to "I notice." This makes your message more neutral, and it causes the child to draw forth inside. When you focus on effort, improvements, contribution, enjoyment, and confidence for the child's experience, that helps you to use encouraging words. The author offers concrete examples of both praise and encouragement.]

- 31) Hammond, Claudia. (2014). Is Praising a Child Good or Bad for Them? *BBC Future*. February 4.

    [We tend to assume that we all enjoy receiving praise, and that it will motivate us to try harder. But when you look at the evidence, it is not that straightforward. The problem may not be the praise, itself, but inflated praise, words like "amazing," "incredible." The author claims that parents are more likely to deliver inflated praise if their child is low in self-confidence hoping it will boost their self-esteem. Praising a child's intelligence can teach them that this human factor is a fixed trait that cannot be controlled, thus negating the impact of effort over cleverness.]

- 32) Hargis, A. (2017). The Peril of Praise. *Child Development Institute of the Redwoods*. May 25.

    [Within a home a parent, without knowing it, may be setting up his or her kids for failed relationships by using overt or covert messages to one child that, through the delivery of selective praise, pits him or her against a sibling.]

- 33) Hoefle, Vicki. (n.d.). The Difference Between Praise and Encouragement. *PBDSparents*. May 14.

    [Some of the problems with praise include perfection rather than progress, and stressing a right or wrong outcome over decision-making. After decades of study to the contrary, parents continue to rely upon praise. The author concludes that she now views encouragement as a way of being.]

- 34) Kastner, Laura. (2016). The Pitfalls of Praising Your Kids. *ParentMap*. October 21.

[Like most parenting trends, we have the first big discovery and then, later, find that there are some kinks in the research. Bolstering self-esteem by lavish praise is an example. Self-esteem, note the word "self," results from substantive effort and commitment on one's part.]

- 35) Kohn, Alfie. (2001). Five Reasons to Stop Saying "Good Job." *Young Children.* 56(5):24-28.

  [Kohn offers five reasons, often repeated in his many other books and articles, to stop using praise with young children. Plain and simple, praise manipulates, especially young children who have a need for adult approval. Further, praise reduces achievement and interest in what otherwise may have been a self-motivating endeavor.]

- 36) [Kohn, Alfie. (1993 / 1999 / 2018). *Punished by Rewards: The Trouble with Gold Stars, Incentive Plans, A's, Praise, and Other Bribes.* Boston: Houghton Mifflin.

  [No book, article, position paper would be complete without calling the reader's attention to the groundbreaking work of Alfie Kohn as contained in his book, *Punished by Rewards.* One of his quotations, "Rewards (e.g., praise) and punishment are simply two sides of the same coin and, in the end, neither gets you much" tells it all. He boldly states, and backs up through references to research, that although deceptively attractive, trying to use rewards (e.g., praise) is ineffective in the long run.]

- 37) Larrivee, B. (2002). The Potential Perils of Praise in a Democratic Interactive Classroom. *Action in Teacher Education.* 23(4):77-78.

  [The author argues that teacher praise can undermine the development of values deemed important to a democratic society. She argues that student praise can discourage freedom of expression, promote conformity, and creates students who may measure their worth by their ability to please others.]

- 38) Lowry, Lauren., and Hanen, SLP (???). "Good Job!" Is Praising Young Children A Good Idea? *The Hanen Center.*

  [First came a need to bolster self-esteem. Then came the universal cure-all (just like penicillin) of supplying loads of praise. It did not live up to its promise. Praise manipulates, creates "praise junkies," steals a child pleasure of recognizing his own quality performance, decreases interest in learning, and reduces achievement.]

- 39) Ludden, David. (2017). Praising Children May Encourage Them to Cheat. *Psychology Today*. September 20.

  [The author claims that praise is one of the cheapest forms of reward, yet we seem to value it so highly. In the author's current study, supplying ability praise ("You are so smart!"), sets up a reputation that the receiver of praise then feels compelled to uphold – perhaps by any means available. Even if the child continues to succeed, it is for the wrong reason – bowing to external forces.]

- 40) Martin, David. L. (1977). Your Praise Can Smother Learning. *Learning*. 5(6):43-51.

  [Plain and simple, too much praise from a teacher may lead the child to expect easy rewards and therefore to avoid more challenging tasks. Simple tasks, on the other hand, almost guarantee the continued receiving of praise.]

- 41) Morin, Amy. (2016). 4 Reasons Compliments Make You Cringe. *Psychology Today*. July 7.

  [People with low self-esteem have the most difficulty accepting compliments, yet it is this group that often is bombarded with praise. delivered praise may not line up with the views that a person has for himself, thus this inconsistency may cause a cognitive dissonance. Some people like to keep the bar low because being expected to excel carries with it unwanted pressure. Finally, there is safety in acting humble when receiving praise, saying a simple "Thank you," and moving on as quickly as possible.]

- 42) Murphy, Ann. P., and Allen, Jennifer. (2007). Why Praise Can Be Bad for Kids. abc NEWS. February.

  [Fifth graders were divided into two groups and given a simple IQ test. The first group was told they had done particularly well and that they must be very smart. The second group was told they had done particularly well and that they must have worked very hard. When invited to take a slightly harder test, the "smart" kids were reluctant. However, 90% of the "effort" kids were eager to take it. On a final test, the "effort" group outperformed the "Intelligent" group.]

- 43) Nicholson, Michael. (2012). The Darker Side of Praise. March 23. Blog.

  [Praise is considered to be an extrinsic reward, most often wielded by parents and teachers. The article addresses situations where one (child or adult) might be expecting praise but not receive it. This can create a sense of competition where not everyone will be deemed praiseworthy.]

- 44) Pearson, Catherine. (2014). The Over-Praise Dilemma: When Complimenting Kids Actually Holds Them Back. *HuffPost*. January 23.

  [Stand near any playground, school yard or classroom and listen. You will hear lots of well-intentioned adults delivering inflated praise – most often to those with a low self-esteem. Inflated praise usually has an accompanying adverb as in "incredibly" good.]

- 45) Pleshette, Ann., and Allen, Jennifer. (2007). Why Praise Can Be Bad for Kids. *abcnews.go.com*

  [According to the authors, if you are like most parents (and teachers) you provide praise to your child believing it is the key to their success. You believe your praise can contribute your child's positive self-esteem. If it were only that simple! Unfortunately, the very strategy we have come to rely on, praise, can have some serious consequences.]

- 46) Raeburn, Paul. (2012). Why It's Bad to Praise Children. *Psychologytoday.com*. February 6.

  [Once again, Alfie Kohn's is heavily referenced. Raeburn suggests that children should be taught to distinguish between good and bad work. The problem is, what does the parent say who has just been approached by her small child who is waving a recently colored "painting" (that is the best that I can describe it) in front of her face, saying "Look what I did!" Does she offer praise for probably what is not all that good of a creation?]

- 47) Richards, Emily. (2006). The Best & Worse in Praise. *Instructor*. 116(1):33-35.

  [The author offers some "best" and "worst" tips when delivering praise. One "best" tip is, "Don't wait for them to cross the finish line." Your author, Dr. Tauber, might seek clarification

because what Richards is suggesting is providing encouragement –
something that can be delivered along the way to the finish line.]

- 48) Rimm, Sylvia. (2010). You're the Greatest: When Praise
  Can Cause Problems.
      [The author tries to reconcile two views, "It's important to
  praise your children," and "But sometimes praise can be bad." Not
  an easy task. Several actual scenarios are offered whereby trying
  to get it right regarding the delivery of praise can be daunting.]

- 49) Romain, Alana. (2016). I Stopped Praising My Kids for
  a Week, & This is What I Learned. *Romper*. January 4.
      [What is the right advice for child rearing? At one time
  kids were regularly spanked. Then, it was all about raising a
  child's self-esteem via lavish (yet not always earned) praise. Now
  parents are told not to praise our children too much. The author,
  although heavily praised herself as a child, attempted to not praise
  her 3-year-old twins for a week. The details of this story are worth
  a read.]

- 50) Solter, Aletha. (2017). Do Really Need Praise? *Aware
  Patenting Institute.*
      [The value of this simple publication lies in her not only
  offering appropriate encouragement statements that might be
  delivered to a child, but also in her arranging these supportive
  messages into helpful categories. The categories include, among
  others, "celebrate with the child" and "show sincere interest by
  asking questions."]

- 51) Stenger, Marianne. (2014). When Praising Kids is a Bad
  Thing. *ABC Splash*. July 1.
      [Unearned praise can do more harm than good, especially
  if a child has a low self-esteem. Inflated praise, rather than
  bolstering self-esteem, can contribute to feelings of insecurity.
  Excessive praise may cause a child to worry whether he or she will
  be able to meet those high expectations next time.]

- 52) Stephens, Karen. (2003). Praise: Like Sugar, it should be
  Sprinkled, Not Poured. Part of a training kit from ChildCare
  Information Exchange.
      [Stresses that praise is often delivered as a compliment. It
  is a short and sweet, often supplied, technique. Children
  sometimes get so much praise that without it they refuse to

perform (e.g., behave). Most alarmingly, the author observed that too many children receive too much praise for too little effort.]

- 53) Strahl, Alyssa. (2016). Praise Versus Encouragement in the Preschool Room. October 17.

    [The author cites a video, "Moving Past Praise: Supporting Kids Through Encouragement" (High Scope 2008). The video talked about praise and how it is negative for a child to be praised. The main reasons were that it lessens the child's self-motivation, the child becomes dependent on adult recognition, and it discourages risk taking. Strahl does not fully agree with the video's message. She still believes that children need to be told what they are doing right and doing well – i.e., a need for adult praise.]

- 54) Tauber, Robert T. (1991). Praise: It Beats Getting Hit with a stick. Maybe. ERIC ED329534.

    [The original manuscript had the title as "Praise: It Beats Getting Hit in the Eye with a Stick!" From this original title you readily can pick up on the author's displeasure with supplying praise to children. Educators commonly consider praise to be an example of "positive" reinforcement, but the author challenges the implication of the word "positive." In fact, there are numerous situations where praise is perceived as an evaluation and, thus, is anything else but "positive."]

- 55) Tauber, Robert T. (1991), Praise "Strikes" Out as a Classroom Management Tool. *Contemporary Education*. Spring 1991.

    [Praise, especially damaging praise, it that which goes beyond a simple affirmation that something is correct. "That is the correct answer," is very different from, "That was an awesome response; I am very proud of you!" Praise may be inappropriate when the receiver perceives it as an evaluation. First and foremost, though, praise *IS* an evaluation and most people do not like to be evaluated.]

- 56) Taylor, Jim (2009). Parenting: Don't praise your children! (Psychologytoday.com).

    [Taylor claims that "Good job" not only is the worst kind of praise, it a lazy, worthless, and harmful way to praise! He claims that we deliver it because we mistakenly believe it will bolster self-esteem. Further, because it takes so little brain power to construct, it is an expedient thing to say. Contrary to the beliefs of many parents, young children do not need praise at all. All they need is to have what they are doing highlighted "I see that you figured out how those puzzle pieces fit together."]

- 57) Terada, Youki. (2017). A Troubling Side Effect of Praise. *edutopia*. October 18.

  [Describes how praising may contribute to children cheating. Immediately after playing a card game that could lead to a prize, three groups of 3-year-olds, one praised, one told they did very well, and one not told anything, secretly were watched when the researcher left the room. Sixty percent of the praised children peeked, whereas only 40% of the other children peeked.]

- 58) Ticknor, Lynne. (2007). Why "Good Job!" Can Be Bad News. *PEPparent.org*.

  [Too much praise can turn children into "people pleasers." Praise is conditional whereas encouragement is unconditional. Encouragement contributes to a child's internal motivation to engage in positive behaviors.]

- 59) Trouborst, Tim (2017). The Fine Line Between Flattery and Praise. *Power to Change*. November 15.

  [According to the author, we have all experienced a compliment that didn't feel right. Instead of feeling affirmed by it, you may have felt used by the person complimenting you. Flattery is used to butter people up in order to get something from them. It is a tool that is used to get something from a person rather than an expression of our valuing that person.]

- 60) Tyrrell, Mark. (n.d.). Why Telling People How Wonderful They Are Isn't Always a Good Idea. *unk.com*

  [Praise may not be all that it is "cracked up to be" so says the author. He cites the raising of self-esteem movement of the 1980's and 1990's and questions the belief that "if a little bit of something is good (e.g., praise) then a lot of it simply must be better!" Too often parents and teachers praise children for things that they should do (and as adults will have to do) such as turning up for school (work) on time, meeting deadlines, or not being disruptive.]

- 61) U-GRO. (2017). Praise vs. Encouragement: Understanding the Difference. *U-GRO.com/*. October 11.

[Praise often comes paired with a judgment or evaluation such as "best," or "great." This type of statement invites a comparison with others rather than a self-evaluation of what works and what does not work. For parents and teachers, it can be a challenge to craft praise statements into encouragement statements, but a goal well worth seeking.]

- 62) Underwood, Paul L. (2020). Are you overpraising your child? *The New York Times*. August 13.

    [By the time you have read this far in this book, it must be clear that all of these authors see the need for being cautious when delivering praise. Praise has a possible dark side. The alternative to delivering praise is delivering encouragement. Underwood points out that to effectively deliver encouragement, you must pay close attention to the "process," not simply the "final product," because there are only so many ways that you can say, "You must have worked really hard on that!" Underwood highlights a couple of praise cautions including, "don't praise by comparison," and "praise only what the other person has control over."]

- 63) Unknown (2014). 'When Being Called "Incredibly Good" is Bad for Children. *Association for Psychological Science*. January 2.

    [Strange as it may sound, heaping praise on those feeling less worthy of it can be damaging. Too often heaping is accompanied by inflated praise, further causing possible damage. Those receiving the most inflated praise are usually those with the lowest self-esteem, clearly advertising this fact to all observers.]

- 64) Walton, Alice. G. (2015). Too Much Praise Can Turn Kids into Narcissists, Study Suggests. *Forbes*. May 9.

    [Lately, "Helicopter parenting," the idea of hovering over one's children has come under criticism. The author reports that over evaluation (of one's child) was the largest predictor of developed narcissistic tendencies, yet, had little impact on the child's self-esteem – the very justification that many parents use for bestowing lavish praise.]

AN IMPORTANT FINAL QUESTION!

My question to those who are willing to put the time and energy into delivering praise would be, "Why don't you consider putting all of that time and energy into perfecting your delivery of encouragement?" Finally, stealing a motto from the "Show Me" state of Missouri, show me the evidence in favor of supplying praise over that of supplying encouragement.

LET ME KNOW!

Let me know if you locate additional articles that address the praise versus encouragement controversy. I can always update these resources for other readers. Thank you ahead of time.

Dr. Robert T. Tauber, PhD
307 Taft Court
Elizabethtown, PA 17022
rtt1453@comcast.net

Books by Dr. Robert T. Tauber, PhD

The first set of books are recently published "professional" books – inexpensive, easily read, interesting, a bit fun to read, and immediately useful to parents, teachers, coaches, managers, practitioners, and other professionals!

- ***Projecting Enthusiasm: The Key to Dynamic Presentations for Professionals!***

  Being enthusiastic is not enough. One *MUST* project that enthusiasm. But how?

- ***Delivering Empathy: Fundamental to Successful Leadership!***

  All successful leaders share one skill – they can deliver empathy to any and all audiences.

- ***Praise Less, Encourage More: Judge, Evaluate and Manipulate Less; Fortify, Galvanize, Embolden and Influence More!***

  Praise & encouragement are *NOT* synonyms. Many cautions surround praise. Basically, no cautions exist for encouragement!

- ***Negative Reinforcement & Time-Out: Two POSITIVE Classroom Management Strategies***

  Not 1 in 1000 people know the definition of negative reinforcement! Thus its overlooked & poorly used.

- ***Giving Children the Expectations Advantage: Make the Power of Expectations Work for You!***

  What you expect, you generally get. How can parents and teachers shape these expectations?

- ***Classroom Management: "What A" to "Z" Discipline Strategies: Simple Strategies that WILL Improve Classroom Discipline!***

  These management skills *WILL* improve home & school discipline.

- ***Oral Communication Skills for the Vocational & Technology Workforce: Walk the Walk and Especially Talk the Talk!***

  Vocational & technical workers are *CHEATED* when it comes to this skill.

- ***Using Empathy as Physicians: The What, Why, and How!***

  Patients deserve emphatic doctors. Do you agree?

The next set of books are recently published "personal" books – also inexpensive, easily read, interesting and, at times, contain more than a bit of tongue-and-cheek humor.

- *From Whence We Came: The Tauber Family History in Photos.*
  Author's family through the decades with pictures.

- *Pottery, Quilts, Books, and Inventions: A Couple's Lifetime of Creativity!*
  The authors' (Cecelia and Robert) half-century-old pottery, thankful quilt recipients, readable and useful books, and inventions that can improve the quality of life.

- *Yorkshire Pudding, Castles, B&Bs and Pubs: An American Family's 1984-85 Sabbatical in England!*
  Off we went to England for a year with 18 pieces of luggage. We came back with the luggage and 2 MG-B car fenders!

- *Inheritance? What Inheritance? We spent it on travel, food, and drink!*
  Our children asked why we were saving our money. They said we should spend it. So, we listened to them – we are spending it!

- *Bob's "AUTO" Biography: Are Cars a Reflection of One's Personality?*
  A history of Bob's 40 vehicles from British sports cars to minivans to RVs.

The remaining books are "professional" books that have stood the test of time and continue to be cited in the professional literature – eye-opening, easily read, interesting, and immediately useful.

- *Classroom Management: Sound Theory and Effective Practice* (1st, 2nd, 3rd & 4th ed).
  Note: The 3rd edition was translated into Chinese!

- *Acting Lessons for Teachers: Using Performance Skills in the Classroom.* (1st & 2nd ed).
  Teaching, as well as most professions, must engage, motivate, and inform an audience. But how? This book is regularly cited in the literature.

- *Self-Fulfilling Prophecy: A Practical Guide to Its Use in Education.* (And all other fields)
  First impressions are lasting impressions. You get what you expect – good or bad! Control them or they will control you!

These inexpensive books are available by going to Amazon.com, selecting "books," & then typing in "Robert T. Tauber." Also available as ebooks.

rtt1453@comcast.net

About the Author

Your author, from a blue-collar family, was raised in a western Pennsylvania steel town where praise and, the mistakenly thought to be opposite, punishment, dominated parenting, teaching and coaching styles. If these were the only two choices available, then it is most certainly clear why most kids would have sought the former.

Education was your author's escape from going into the local steel mill where many fathers and grandfathers had worked. Education consisted of a Bachelor of Science degree in physics at a state school, followed by MEd at a nearby university, and a PhD from The Pennsylvania State University. It was while supervising student teachers for Penn State that your author developed his interest in several areas, including how praise and encouragement differ.

Throughout his career your author has focused on several areas. Those areas are reflected in his numerous journal publications and books. Feel free to conduct a Google search using "Robert T. Tauber."

His career involved serving two academic sabbaticals, one at Durham University (England) and one at Melbourne University (Australia) where, among other areas of investigation, he researched the differences between praise and encouragement.